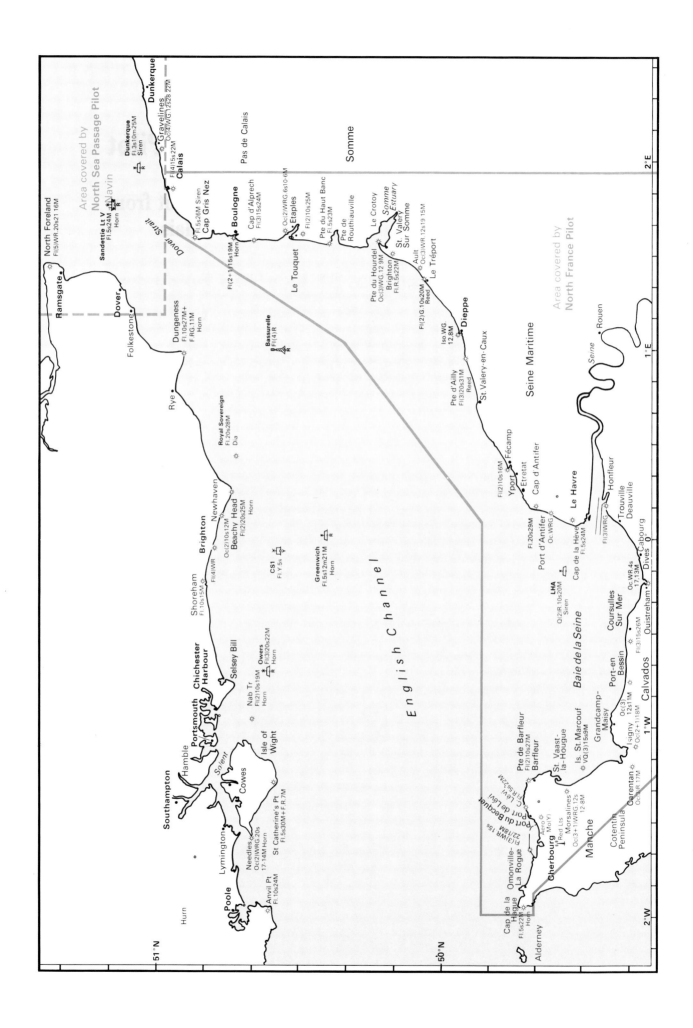

North France Pilot

A YACHTSMAN'S PILOT FROM CHERBOURG TO CALAIS

Trevor and Dinah Thompson

Imray Laurie Norie & Wilson Ltd
St Ives Cambridgeshire England

Published by
Imray, Laurie, Norie & Wilson Ltd
Wych House, St Ives, Huntingdon,
Cambridgeshire, PE17 4BT, England.

British Library Cataloguing in Publication Data

Thompson, Trevor
   North France Pilot.
   1. Northern France. Coastal waters – Pilots' guides
   I. Title   II. Thompson, Dinah
   623.89'29442

   ISBN 0 85288 137 1

CAUTION
Whilst every care has been taken to ensure accuracy, neither the Publishers nor the Authors will hold themselves responsible for errors, omissions or alterations in this publication. They will at all times be grateful to receive information which tends to the improvement of the work.

PLANS
The plans in this guide are not to be used for navigation. They are designed to support the text and should at all times be used with navigational charts.

The last input of technical information was October 1989.

Set in Plantin by Cromwell Graphics Ltd, St Ives, Huntingdon direct from the Authors' and Publishers' disks.

Printed in Great Britain at The Bath Press, Avon

Contents

Preface

A successful landfall in the very French port you had decided on, the first *bonjour*, a crisp *baguette* and a bottle of *vin ordinaire* tucked under your arm, the promise of buttery croissants for breakfast, and that indefinable smell which is France – what a way to start a cruise along this northern coast of France. You have arrived and the delights of France await you.

The north coast of France is so near and accessible to many British yachtsmen, yet it is so very foreign and different. Making contact with the French people, and getting to grips with their language, culture and cuisine give an added dimension to the normal cruising challenges of wind and tides, navigation and know-how.

As youngsters we had both been to France on numerous family holidays, and, in the manner of the very young, were blasé about going foreign. When we came to sail *Joleta of Pettycur* across to France for the first time, we were caught unawares by the exhilaration of our first foreign-going voyage. That sense of adventure has been with us on all subsequent trips to France.

The north coast of France, between Cherbourg and Calais, is an area of contrasts. There are cliffs and rocks, low marshy areas, estuaries, and long sandy beaches. The harbours range from large commercial ports such as Le Havre and Cherbourg, to sophisticated marinas such as Deauville, and small fishing ports such as Le Hourdel. This is a popular yachting area with the French, so all the facilities are available. Despite that it is still possible to find a quiet berth for the night.

The coast is studded with villages and towns which have been developed to cater for holidaymakers. This means that there is a good choice of restaurants, sports facilities, museums and other places of interest. If you have to stay in harbour because of bad weather there is plenty to do and see in most places, both for adults and children.

We hope that this pilot will be of assistance to all yachtsmen going to this part of France, particularly those who have not yet ventured across the Channel. We have been very careful in seeking out and checking the information given, which has then been checked again by the Publishers. If, however, when you use this pilot you find that things have changed or an error has been made please let us know, through the Publishers, so that other users may benefit.

We would like to take this opportunity to thank William and Alison Wilson and the staff at Imray Laurie Norie & Wilson for their unfailing help and encouragement, and Nell Stuart for editing and checking our manuscript. Our thanks are also due to the yachtsmen who gave us the benefit of their experience in cruising this area, George Taylor, Editor of *Practical Boat Owner*, the staff in various French tourist offices who patiently answered our questions, often phrased in the most appalling French, and to Gordon Lucking, Maureen Butcher and all the staff at G. H. Lucking & Sons Ltd who made the time available for yet another long cruise. Finally we wish to record our gratitude to the late Mrs Vera Young who kindly kept an eye on our cottage and garden whilst we were away on our travels. Without the help and encouragement we have received this project might never have got off the ground, and it would certainly not have been as much fun.

Trevor and Dinah Thompson
Washington, Sussex 1989

DEDICATION

To Bill and Mary Lyons

Introduction

At its nearest point (Cap Gris Nez) the north coast of France is barely 20 miles away from the English coast, and, on a good day, is clearly visible.

Separating England from France is the English Channel (La Manche to the French). This natural barrier with its strong tides and sandbanks has saved England from the many invasions to which France has been subject over the centuries. Despite many attempts at the invasion of England few have been successful. The most notable successes were Julius Caesar's invasion in 33 BC and William the Conqueror's invasion in 1066.

William the Conqueror, the Duke of Normandy, started a long formal connection between England and northern France. Indeed during the Middle Ages the kings of England ruled large tracts of what is now France. Many of the harbours on this northern coast of France have historic links with England. Barfleur, Caen, Dives, St-Valéry-sur-Somme, all have some link with William the Conqueror. Calais belonged to the English crown until lost during the reign of Mary Tudor. It was off Barfleur in 1120 that the *White Ship*, carrying the heir of Henry I, was shipwrecked, so leading to the war between Queen Matilda and Stephen. In more recent times the 'mulberry' harbour of Arromanches was a creation of Winston Churchill and contributed to the success of the Allied invasion of Europe and the defeat of Hitler.

Today the yachtsman is perhaps going to have less regard for the historic role of the Channel. He is going to be more concerned with the problems of crossing the shipping lanes and worried about the possibility of fog or strong winds. The English Channel is the busiest stretch of water in the world with an estimated one ship every minute passing through the Dover Strait. This concentration of shipping has led to the introduction and strict enforcement of shipping lanes.

Once across the Channel the British yachtsman will find much that is familiar along with all that is foreign. The north coast of France has much to offer the visitor. Yachtsmen are well catered for and welcome in most harbours, even the fishing and ferry ports. There is some beautiful countryside, a wealth of fascinating museums and castles, and of course delicious food and fine wines.

Stocking up with duty-free items is no problem in the major ports such as Cherbourg and Calais. The British yachtsman wanting to fill his bilges with cheap beer, wines and spirits, is not considered to be a nuisance in France; unlike the attitude he may experience on the other side of the Channel!

There are sufficient contrasts of scenery and challenges of navigation to prevent boredom when sailing along this coast. At one extreme you have the Cotentin peninsula, with its offlying reefs, rocks and tidal races, to keep you on your toes. The sandy and shallow estuaries with their shifting channels, such as the Somme estuary, demand a different type of skill. Then you have the alabaster chalk cliffs of the Pays de Caux where it can be difficult to locate the harbours, but where the white cliffs look so attractive against a turquoise sea and an azure sky.

We hope that your cruises along this northern coast of France are marked by fair winds, a friendly reception and a sense of fun.

How to use this book

Geographical coordinates
The latitude and longitude given for each port represent the approximate position of the harbour entrance, rounded to the nearest minute. They are quoted to help you locate the ports on your chart. If using a satellite navigation or Decca system you cannot aim for the quoted coordinates and expect to pass through the centre of the harbour entrance.

Wind and tidal stream directions
Winds are described by the direction from which they blow, and tidal streams by the direction towards which they flow.

Key to symbols and abbreviations

	Port office
⚓	Harbourmaster
🕱	Water
🕯	Fuel
⌐	Crane
✉	Post office
☎	Telephone
⬚	Travel-lift
V	Visitors' berths
►	Yacht club
⊖	Customs
⚓	Anchoring prohibited

Distances
Distances are given in nautical miles or cables (tenths of a nautical mile).

Depths
Depths are given in metres below chart datum.

Heights
Heights are given in metres above MHWS.

Bearings and abbreviations
The bearings given are all in 360° notation and are true. On the plans north is indicated by the capital letter N.

The English Channel

In this pilot we are concerned with the stretch of the English Channel between Cap de la Hague in the west and Calais in the east.

Natural hazards
The main natural hazards in this area are a series of sandbanks which generally lie towards the east and middle of the Channel and parallel to the French coast. Some of these sandbanks have less than 1m over them in places. They are well marked, but because of the possibility of fog or bad weather attention to navigation at all times is important.

Various rocks and reefs are to be found close to some parts of the English and French coasts. The Cotentin peninsula is particularly rocky with some rocks and reefs lying nearly 2 miles offshore. The Plateau du Calvados, a line of rocks, lies off the coast between Arromanches and Ouistreham. In this area shallow water extends approximately 4 miles offshore.

For details of the natural hazards along the French coast please refer to the pilotage section.

Wrecks
There are numerous dangerous wrecks lying off the French coast, particularly in the area of the Normandy Landing beaches and between Le Tréport and Calais. Note that a number of these wrecks are dangerous to yachts. Some are close to the surface and some are not marked by buoys. It is therefore essential to check the relevant chart.

Other hazards
This is an extremely busy area for shipping. Merchant ships, naval vessels, ferries, fishing boats, and supertankers, not to mention yachts, may all be seen. Yachts should keep a good lookout at all times, and should in particular give the supertankers a wide berth. Supertankers are restricted in their ability to manoeuvre, and for instance, in some sections of the Dover Strait their draught is such that they may be uncomfortably close to the bottom. Their mass is so large that they will take 10 miles to stop, and 2 miles to answer the helm.

Cross-Channel ferries and hovercraft will also be encountered. At times sighting a ferry can be a useful aid to navigation when you can't quite work out where the harbour entrance is! Care should however be exercised when entering or leaving a ferry port. It is not always possible to see a ferry approaching the other side of a harbour entrance from the deck of a yacht.

Fishing boats operate from most ports along the French and English coasts. Most of them are trawlers, and they should be given a wide berth. Beware of lobster pots on both sides of the Channel. The floats and markers are often difficult to see, especially if there is a strong tide running, if it is dark, or the sea rough.

Occasionally cable-laying operations or oceanographic surveys are undertaken. Red painted guard ships may be on duty around such operations and will warn vessels away. Any unusual activity of this nature will be announced by *Notices to Mariners* or by the Channel Navigation Information Service.

The Lieutenance, formerly the residence of the French king's governor in Honfleur and one of Honfleur's most famous buildings, stands at the entrance to the Vieux Bassin.

Navigational aids

Buoyage

IALA System A is in use on both sides of the English Channel. The direction of buoyage is from southwest to northeast. In the approaches to harbours and estuaries the direction of buoyage is generally from seaward; i.e. red can buoys are left to port, green conical buoys are left to starboard.

Major lights

The following are the major lights on the north coast of France between Cap de la Hague and Calais.

Name of light	Characteristics	Fog signal	Position
Cap de la Hague	Fl.5s48m23M	Horn 30s	49°43′·4N 1°57′·3W
Cherbourg (Fort de l'Ouest)	Fl(3)WR.15s19m22/18M	Reed(3)60s	49°40′·5N 1°38′·9W
Cap Lévi	Fl.R.5s36m22M		49°41′·8N 1°28′·4W
Pointe de Barfleur-Gatteville	Fl(2)10s72m29M	Reed(2)60s	49°41′·8N 1°15′·9W
Iles Saint-Marcouf-Ile du Large	VQ(3)5s18m9M		49°29′·9N 1°08′·8W
Carentan Ldg Lts 210°	DirOc(3)R.12s6m17M Oc(3)12s14m11M		49°20′·5N 1°11′·2W
Isigny Ldg Lts 172·5°	DirOc(2+1)12s7m18M DirOc(2+1)12s19m18M		49°19′·6N 1°06′·8W
Grandcamp	Oc.4s8m13M		49°23′·4N 1°02′·5W
Ver	Fl(3)15s42m26M		49°20′·5N 0°31′·1W
Ouistreham	Oc.WR.4s37m17/13M		49°16′·8N 0°14′·9W
Le Havre Ldg Lts 107°			
Lower light	DirF.36m25M		49°29′·0N 0°06′·5E
Upper light	DirF.78m25M		49°28′·8N 0°07′·6E
Le Havre Digue Nord	Fl.R.5s15m21M	Horn 15s	49°29′·2N 0°05′·4E
Cap de la Hève	Fl.5s123m24M		49°30′·8N 0°04′·1E
LHA lanby	Q(2)R.10s10m20M		49°31′·7N 0°09′·9W
Cap d'Antifer	Fl.20s128m29M		49°41′·1N 0°09′·9E
Fécamp	Fl(2)10s15m16M	Reed(2)30s	49°46′·0N 0°21′·8E
Pointe d'Ailly	Fl(3)20s95m31M	Horn(3)60s	49°55′·0N 0°57′·6E
Le Tréport (Jetée Ouest)	Fl(2)G.10s15m20M	Reed Mo(N)30s	50°03′·9N 1°22′·2E
Ault	Oc(3)WR.12s95m18/14M		50°06′·3N 1°27′·2E
Pointe du Hourdel	Oc(3)WG.12s19m12/9M	Reed(3)30s	50°12′·9N 1°34′·0E
Cayeux-sur-Mer (Brighton)	Fl.R.5s32m22M		50°11′·7N 1°30′·7E
Point du Haut-Banc	Fl.5s44m23M		50°23′·9N 1°33′·7E
Le Touquet-Paris-Plage	Fl(2)10s54m25M		50°31′·4N 1°35′·6E
Cap d'Alprech	Fl(3)15s62m24M		50°42′·0N 1°33′·8E
Boulogne (Digue Sud)	Fl(2+1)15s25m19M		50°44′·5N 1°34′·1E
Cap Gris Nez	Fl.5s72m29M	Siren 60s	50°52′·2N 1°35′·0E
Calais (Jetée Est)	Fl(2)R.6s12m17M	Reed(2)40s	50°58′·4N 1°50′·5E
Calais (Main Lt)	Fl(4)15s59m23M		50°57′·7N 1°51′·2E

VHF radio lighthouses

The following are the VHF radio lighthouses in this area, operating on Ch 88. For details of their use refer to your nautical almanac or the *Admiralty List of Radio Signals Volume 2*.

Name	Ident.	Position
Anvil Point	AL	50°35′·5N 1°57′·5W
High Down, Scratchells Bay	HD	50°39′·7N 1°34′·6W
Calais main light	CL	50°57′·7N 1°51′·3E

Radiobeacons

This area is well served by marine radiobeacons. There are also some air radiobeacons which can be useful, with caution.

Name	Ident.	Freq. (kHz)	Range (miles)	Seq.	Position
Marine radiobeacons					
England					
Portland Bill	PB	291·9	50	1	50°30'·8N 2°27'·3W
Poole Harbour	PO	303·4	10	3, 6	50°41'·0N 1°56'·7W
St Catherine's Point	CP	291·9	50	2	50°34'·5N 1°17'·8W
Nab Lt	NB	312·6	10	1, 3, 5	50°40'·1N 0°57'·1W
Chichester Bar Bn	CH	303·4	10	1, 4	50°45'·9N 0°56'·4W
Brighton Marina	BM	303·4	10	2, 5	50°48'·7N 0°06'·0W
Newhaven	NH	303·4	10	3, 6	50°46'·9N 0°03'·5E
Royal Sovereign	RY	310·3	50	2	50°43'·4N 0°26'·2E
Dungeness	DU	310·3	30	6	50°54'·8N 0°58'·7E
France					
Cherbourg	RB	312·6	20	2, 4, 6	49°40'·5N 1°38'·9W
Pointe de Barfleur	FG	291·9	70	6	49°41'·9N 1°15'·9W
Port-en-Bessin	BS	313·5	5	H24	49°21'·0N 0°45'·6W
Pointe de Ver	ER	291·9	20	5	49°20'·5N 0°31'·2W
LHA Lanby	LH	291·9	30	4	49°31'·7N 0°09'·8W
Cap d'Antifer	TI	291·9	50	3	49°41'·1N 0°10'·0E
Pointe d'Ailly	AL	310·3	50	4	49°55'·0N 0°57'·6E
Cap d'Alprech	PH	310·3	20	1, 3, 5	50°42'·0N 1°33'·8E
Calais	CS	305·7	20	5	50°57'·7N 1°51'·3E
Air radiobeacons					
England					
Alderney	ALD	383	50	H24	49°42'·6N 2°11'·9W
Hurn (Bournemouth)	HRN	394	35	H24	50°48'·0N 1°43'·7W
Fawley/Hythe	FAW	370	20	H24	51°52'·0N 1°23'·4W
France					
Le Touquet	LT	358	20	H24	50°32'·1N 1°35'·4E
Le Havre/Octeville	LHO	346	15	H24	49°35'·8N 0°11'·0E
Calais/Dunkerque	MK	275	15	H24	50°59'·9N 2°03'·3E

Coast radio stations

England	*VHF working channels*
Jersey Radio	25, 82
Weymouth Bay Radio	05
Niton Radio	28, 81, 85
N Foreland Radio	05, 26, 65, 66
Hastings Radio	07, 63
France	
Cherbourg	27
Port-en-Bessin	03
Rouen	25, 27
Le Havre	23, 26, 28
Dieppe Radio	02, 24
Boulogne Radio	23, 25
Calais Radio	01, 87
Dunkerque Radio	24, 61

Channel Navigation Information Service (CNIS)

The Channel Navigation Information Service broadcasts navigational information for the Dover Strait area. For example it may give information on a vessel passing through the Dover Strait which is restricted in its ability to manoeuvre, or it may report the non-functioning of a light, or a buoy out of position.

Another function of the Channel Navigation Information Service is to check that vessels within its area are complying with Rule 10 of the *International Regulations for Preventing Collisions at Sea* (see page 9 for Rule 10). A vessel breaking the rules may be identified by a light aircraft, helicopter or ship.

CNIS broadcasts on VHF Ch 16 and 69. Information broadcasts are on VHF Ch 11 at every hour +40. If visibility is less than 2 miles it also broadcasts at every hour +55.

French port traffic signals

Entry and departure from some French ports are regulated by a system of traffic lights. There are two systems in use: a full code which is used in major ports, and a simplified code used in the smaller ports (see diagram for details).

Port traffic signals

Meaning	*Day*	*Night*
Port closed – entry strictly prohibited (on account of a serious problem)	● R ● R ● R	☼ R ☼ R ☼ R
Port open – but there may be obstructions in the channels, so proceed with caution		☼ G ☼ G ☼ G

	Full code		*Simplified code*	
Meaning	*Day*	*Night*	*Day*	*Night*
Entrance prohibited	● ▲ ●	☼ R ☼ W ☼ R	▨ R	☼ R
Departure prohibited	▼ ▲ ▼	☼ G ☼ W ☼ G	▨ G	☼ G
Entrance and departure prohibited	▼ ▲ ●	☼ G ☼ W ☼ R	▨ R ▨ G	☼ R ☼ G

Weather

The summer weather in this area is characterised by light to moderate west to southwest winds. There are occasional periods of strong winds, possibly reaching gale force, which can last for some days at a time. British and French shipping forecasts usually provide timely and accurate warning of adverse conditions.

In certain areas geographical features can influence the weather locally. For example, the Cotentin peninsula with Cherbourg at its centre, has the effect of accelerating the wind strength by perhaps one force on the Beaufort scale. The generally straight coastline in the vicinity of Dieppe also tends to strengthen the prevailing westerly winds. In the Dover Strait the wind is funnelled through a narrowing gap which increases the wind strength to up to 20% greater than the barometric pressure wind.

During the summer months there may be thunderstorms over France which can move northwards across the Channel in the direction of England. These thunderstorms are more likely to occur at night and are often accompanied by violent squalls.

While visibility is often good, fog and poor visibility may be encountered even in the summer.

Weather forecasts

Local time

In Britain summer time starts on the last Sunday in March and ends on the last Sunday in October. Summer time = UT (Universal Time) +1 hour.

In France winter (or standard) time = UT +1 hour. Summer time = UT +2 hours. French summer time starts on the last Sunday in March and ends on the last Sunday in September. UT is called *Temps Universal* or TU in France; local time is *l'heure locale*.

English coast radio stations

Frequent and generally accurate weather forecasts are easily available in both British and French waters. British sea areas Wight and Dover apply to the area covered by this pilot.

The main shipping forecast is broadcast by the BBC Radio 4 (198 kHz, 1515m) at 0033, 0555, 1355, and 1750 (local British time). There is also a useful inshore forecast broadcast by BBC Radio 3 on 1215 kHz, 247m, at 0655 (local British time).

The shipping forecast is broadcast by the British coast radio stations as follows.

Station	VHF Ch	Times (UT)	Sea Areas
Jersey	25, 82	0645, 0745, 1245, 1845, 2245	Channel Islands south of 50°N and east of 3°W and French coast
Weymouth Bay	05	0833, 2033	Dover, Wight, Portland
Niton	28	0733, 1933	Dover, Wight, Portland
Hastings	07	0803, 2003	Humber, Thames, Dover, Wight
North Foreland	26	0733, 1933	Thames, Dover, Wight

Marinecall

Another source of up-to-date weather information is offered by *Marinecall*. By dialling the appropriate number you gain access to a recorded weather forecast. *Marinecall* is operated by Telephone Information Services Ltd using information from the Meteorological office. The forecast is available 24 hours a day, 7 days a week, and is updated three times a day in the summer. It gives information for up to 12 miles off the coast, and can also give information on Channel crossing routes. ☎ (0898) 500 456 for a weather forecast for the Channel East area (Selsey Bill to North Foreland, plus the French coast from Le Havre to Calais), or ☎ (0898) 500 457 for the Mid-Channel area (Lyme Regis to Selsey Bill, plus the Channel Islands and the Cherbourg peninsula. For a 3 to 5-day forecast ☎ (0898) 500 450.

The coastguard broadcasts the *Marinecall* forecast on VHF Ch 67 at regular intervals. In practice we have managed to hear these broadcasts when 30 miles off the British coast.

French coast radio stations

The French forecast areas of relevance to this pilot are Manche Est and Dover. In France you will find the forecasts (written in French) posted up at marina and port offices. These are easy to understand, even with only a rudimentary knowledge of French. Unfortunately this is not the case with the weather forecasts broadcast by the French coast radio stations. Their forecasts are given in French only, and at a fairly rapid rate. Details of these broadcasts are as follows; each one covers the sea area from Cap de la Hague to the Belgian border.

Station	VHF Ch	Times (UT)
Cherbourg	27	0633, 1133
Port-en-Bessin	03	0633, 1133
Le Havre	26	0633, 1133
Dieppe	02	0633, 1133
Boulogne	23	0633, 1133
Calais	87	0633, 1133
Dunkerque	61	0633, 1133

All of these forecasts are broadcast 1 hour earlier when Daylight Saving Time is in force; i.e. the 1133 broadcast in summer is actually at 1133 British Summer Time (1233 local French time).

Répondeurs automatiques

Various French meteorological stations provide recorded weather forecasts which can be obtained by dialling the following numbers:

Cherbourg	☎ 33 43 20 40
Deauville	☎ 31 88 84 22
Caen	☎ 31 75 14 14
Rouen	☎ 35 80 11 44
Le Havre	☎ 35 21 16 11
Le Touquet	☎ 21 05 13 55
Boulogne	☎ 21 33 82 55
Dunkerque	☎ 28 63 44 44

French coastguard stations

The French navy maintains coast signal stations, or *sémaphores*, which carry out similar duties to the British coastguard service. They monitor shipping movements within their area, keeping a visual, radio and radar watch. Certain signal stations, however, are only manned between sunrise and sunset. Should a vessel require assistance the signal station will relay a message to the relevant rescue service.

Signal stations display storm warnings. In addition weather forecasts will be repeated on request by radio or telephone. The telephone numbers of the signal stations in this area are as follows:

La Hague[1]	☎ 33 52 71 07
Le Homet	☎ 33 92 60 08
Lévi[1]	☎ 33 54 31 17
Barfleur	☎ 33 54 04 37
Saint Vaast[1]	☎ 33 54 44 50
Port-en-Bessin	☎ 31 21 81 51
Villerville[1]	☎ 31 88 11 13
La Hève	☎ 35 46 07 81
Fécamp[1]	☎ 35 28 00 91
Dieppe[1]	☎ 35 84 23 82
Ault[1]	☎ 22 60 47 33
Boulogne[1]	☎ 21 31 32 10
Dunkerque	☎ 28 66 86 18

Note
1. Signal station only manned sunrise to sunset.

French terms used in weather forecasts

French	English
prévisions météo	weather forecasts
abondant	heavy
affaiblissement	decrease
agité(e)	rough
amélioration	improvement
anticyclone	anticyclone
après midi	afternoon
augmentant	increasing
aujourd'hui	today
averse	shower
avis	warning
avis de coup de vent	gale warning
basse pression	low pressure
en baisse	falling
banc de brouillard	fog bank
beau	fair, fine
belle (mer)	smooth
bon(ne)	good
en bordure	on the border, edge of
brouillard	fog
brise	breeze
brise de mer	sea breeze
brise de terre	land breeze
bruine	drizzle
brume légère	haze
brume mouillée	mist
brume sèche	haze
brumeux	misty, foggy
calme	calm
centre	centre
comblant	filling
coup de vent	gale
courant	current
couvert	overcast
creusant	deepening
cyclonique	cyclonic
demain	tomorrow
se déplaçant	moving
dépression (bas)	depression (low)
direction	direction
se dispersant	dispersing
dorsale	ridge
éclair	lightning
éclaircie	bright interval
échelle de Beaufort	Beaufort scale
état de la mer	sea state
est	east
étendu	extensive
extension	extending
faible	slight, weak
force du vent	wind force
en formation	building
fort	strong
fraîche	fresh
frais	fresh
fréquent	frequent
front	front
front froid	cold front
front chaud	warm front
gelée	frost
grain	squall
grand frais	near gale
grêle	hail
en hausse	rising
haut	high
houle	swell
isolé	isolated
jour, journée	day
au large	at sea
léger	light
légère	light
légèrement	lightly
lentement	slowly
locale	local
matin	morning
mauvais	poor
même	the same
mer	sea
mer forte	rough sea
modéré	moderate
se modérant	moderating
neige et pluie	sleet
noeuds	knots
nord	north
nuages	clouds
nuageux	cloudy
nuit	night
orage	thunderstorm
orageux	stormy
ouest	west
ouragan	hurricane
passagèrement	temporarily
perturbation	disturbance
pluie	rain
précipitation	precipitation
pression	pressure
prévision	forecast
probabilité	probability, chances of
profond	deep
rapidement	quickly
rafale	gust
recul du vent	backing
région	area
ressac	surge, backwash
rester, restant	remain, stay
sans nuages	cloudless
situation générale	general synopsis
suivant	following
sporadiques	scattered
stationnaire	stationary
sud	south
temps	weather, time
tempête	storm
tonnerre	thunder
vagues	waves
variable	variable
vent	wind
vent frais	strong breeze
vent à rafales	gusty
virement	veering
visibilité	visibility
zone	area

Numerals

1	*un*	20	*vingt*
2	*deux*	21	*vingt et un*
3	*trois*	22	*vingt-deux*
4	*quatre*	30	*trente*
5	*cinq*	40	*quarante*
6	*six*	50	*cinquante*
7	*sept*	60	*soixante*
8	*huit*	70	*soixante-dix*
9	*neuf*	80	*quatre-vingt*
10	*dix*	90	*quatre-vingt-dix*
11	*onze*	99	*quatre-vingt-dix-neuf*
12	*douze*	100	*cent*
13	*treize*	101	*cent un*
14	*quatorze*	110	*cent dix*
15	*quinze*	182	*cent quatre-vingt-deux*
16	*seize*	200	*deux cents*
17	*dix-sept*	307	*trois cent sept*
18	*dix-huit*	1000	*mille*
19	*dix-neuf*	1002	*mille deux*

Wind strength

The Beaufort scale is being used increasingly in French weather forecasts, especially on the Channel coast. Occasionally however the wind strength is given in metres per second.

Beaufort scale	Metres per second
Force 0	0–0·2
Force 1	0·3–1·5
Force 2	1·6–3·3
Force 3	3·4–5·4
Force 4	5·5–7·9
Force 5	8·0–10·7
Force 6	10·8–13·8
Force 7	13·9–17·1
Force 8	17·2–20·7
Force 9	20·8–24·4
Force 10	24·5–28·4
Force 11	28·5–32·6
Force 12	32·7 plus

Sea

Tides

Tides in the English Channel flow from southwest to northeast on the flood and in the reverse direction on the ebb. Maximum rates are reached off headlands and promontories such as the Cotentin peninsula where the tide can attain in excess of 4 knots. Tidal range can be as much as 6 metres on springs (Calais) or as little as 2·5 metres on neaps (Cherbourg).

Sea state

Wind-over-tide conditions can create uncomfortable if not dangerous seas in even moderate winds. Under these conditions tidal races, such as the Raz de Barfleur, and areas of strong tidal streams should be avoided. The following French terms are used to describe sea state (*état de la mer*):

French term	Wave height
calme	0m
calme (ridée)	0·1m
belle	0·1–0·5m
peu agitée	0·5–1·25m
agitée	1·25–2·5m
forte	2·5–4
très forte	4–6m
grosse	6–9m
très grosse	9–14m
énorme	over 14m
	Swell
houle petite	under 2m
houle modérée	2–4m
houle grande	over 4m

Charts and publications

Not surprisingly this area is well covered by charts and pilot books. The British charts are excellent and have the advantage that in Britain they are easily available. We have made extensive use of British Admiralty charts as well as Imray's yachting charts. The French yachtsmen's charts, *Carte Guide de Navigation Côtière*, and French naval charts can be purchased from French chandlers, some French book shops, or by post from Imrays and other British chart agents such as Kelvin Hughes in London. In most instances the British charts will be more than adequate, but for certain areas, such as the 'mulberry' harbour of Arromanches, the local French charts are preferable. Be warned however that the symbols, etc. are different. For a detailed list of chart titles and scales see Appendix II.

General charts (for passage-making)
Admiralty *2656, 2612, 2450, 2451, 2613, 2669*
Imray *C12, C30, C31, C32, C33A, C8*

Detailed charts
Admiralty *2994, 1106, 2073, 1821, 2146, 2147, 1892, 323*

Harbour plans
Admiralty *2602, 1349, 2990, 1352, 438, 2147*
Imray charts include the harbour plans

Admiralty pilots
NP28 *Dover Strait Pilot*
NP27 *Channel Pilot*

Tidal atlases
Admiralty NP 233 *Dover Strait*, NP 250 *English and Bristol Channels*
Stanford *English Channel East, English Channel West*

Light lists
NP74 *Admiralty List of Lights, Vol. A*

Almanacs

The Macmillan & Silk Cut Nautical Almanac
Practical Boat Owner Cruising Almanac
Reed's Nautical Almanac

Other pilots

Cruising Association Handbook
The Shell Pilot to the English Channel, Vol. 2, John
    Coote, Faber and Faber
Normandy and Channel Islands Pilot, Mark Bracken-
    bury, Adlard Coles Ltd
Inland Waterways of France, David Edwards-May,
    Imray, Laurie, Norie and Wilson Ltd
A Cruising Guide to the Lower Seine, E. L. Howells,
    Imray, Laurie, Norie and Wilson Ltd
Votre Livre du Bord, Manche et Atlantique, Bloc
    Marin

Life saving

In France lifeboats are maintained by the Société
Nationale de Sauvetage en Mer. The French equi-
valent of H. M. Coastguard Maritime Rescue Coor-
dination Centres are called CROSS – Centres
Régionaux Opérationnels de Surveillance et de
Sauvetage. There are various centres around the
coast. The two of interest to yachtsmen sailing
within the area covered by this pilot are CROSS
Jobourg, which covers the area from Le Mont-St-
Michel to Cap d'Antifer (☎ 33 52 72 13), and
CROSS Gris-Nez, which covers the area from Cap
d'Antifer to the Belgian frontier (☎ 21 87 21 87).

At many ports you will be given a form by the
harbour or marina authorities which is to be completed and returned before departure. The form,
Avis de Passage, printed in French and English, asks
for details of the vessel, crew, next-of-kin and the
next two ports of call. Should you get into diffi-
culties or be reported missing the form is intended
to help the authorities find you. It is similar to the
procedure operated by H. M. Coastguard, and like
the British system is not compulsory.

Crossing the shipping lanes

To prevent collisions between vessels using the English Channel, traffic separation zones and shipping
lanes have been created. The ones which lie within
the area of this pilot are shown on the diagram on
page 14. In each lane the traffic flows in one direction only. There are inshore zones where the traffic
can be going in any direction. You are also likely to
encounter fishing boats and fishing floats in these
inshore zones. Fishing boats may also be encountered in the separation zones.

Vessels must cross the shipping lanes at right
angles. To do this slow-moving vessels such as sailing yachts must maintain a heading as nearly as possible at right angles to the traffic flow in the lane.
You should not make an allowance for the tide if by
doing so would mean heading at an angle other than
90° to the flow of traffic.

Rule 10 of the *International Regulations for Preventing Collisions at Sea* covers the separation
schemes. Because it is so important it is quoted in
full here.

Rule 10 Traffic Separation Schemes

a. This Rule applies to traffic separation schemes
   adopted by the Organisation.
b. A vessel using a traffic separation scheme shall:
   i. proceed in the appropriate traffic lane in the
      general direction of traffic flow for that lane;
   ii. so far as practicable keep clear of a traffic
      separation line or separation zone;
   iii.normally join or leave a traffic lane at the
      termination of the lane, but when joining or
      leaving from either side shall do so at as small
      an angle to the general direction of traffic flow
      as practicable.
c. A vessel shall so far as practicable avoid crossing
   traffic lanes, but if obliged to do so shall cross as
   nearly as practicable at right angles to the general
   direction of traffic flow.
d. Inshore traffic zones shall not normally be used
   by through traffic which can safely use the appropriate traffic lane within the adjacent traffic
   separation scheme. However, vessels of less than
   20 metres in length and sailing vessels may under
   all circumstances use inshore traffic zones.
e. A vessel, other than a crossing vessel or a vessel
   joining or leaving a lane, shall not normally enter
   a separation zone or cross a separation line except:
   i. in cases of emergency to avoid immediate
      danger;
   ii. to engage in fishing within a separation zone.
f. A vessel navigating in areas near the terminations
   of traffic separation schemes shall do so with particular caution.
g. A vessel shall so far as practicable avoid anchoring in a traffic separation scheme or in areas near
   its terminations.
h. A vessel not using a traffic separation scheme
   shall avoid it by as wide a margin as is practicable.
i. A vessel engaged in fishing shall not impede the
   passage of any vessel following a traffic lane.
j. A vessel of less than 20 metres in length or a sailing vessel shall not impede the safe passage of a
   power-driven vessel following a traffic lane.
k. A vessel restricted in her ability to manoeuvre
   when engaged in an operation for the maintenance of safety of navigation in a traffic separation scheme is exempted from complying with
   this Rule to the extent necessary to carry out the
   operation.
l. A vessel restricted in her ability to manoeuvre
   when engaged in an operation for the laying, ser-
   vicing or picking up of a submarine cable, within
   a traffic separation scheme, is exempted from
   complying with this Rule to the extent necessary
   to carry out the operation.

Communications

Bus services

Most of the French ports described in this pilot are linked to neighbouring towns and villages by a bus service. The local tourist information office will be able to provide you with details of the services available and the timetable.

Rail

France has an excellent rail system. There are railway stations at the following ports: Cherbourg, Carentan, Caen, Dives, Deauville-Trouville, Le Havre, Fécamp, St-Valéry-en-Caux, Dieppe, Le Tréport, Etaples, Boulogne and Calais. Note that before getting on the train you must validate (*composter*) your ticket by using the orange automatic date-stamping machine which will be found at the entrance to the platform. If you do not validate your ticket you will have to pay a surcharge.

Ferries and hovercraft

Conveniently for the yachtsman the north coast of France has excellent ferry and hovercraft links with England. Ferries operate between the following ports:
Cherbourg and Weymouth
Cherbourg and Poole
Cherbourg and Portsmouth
Ouistreham and Portsmouth
Le Havre and Portsmouth
Dieppe and Newhaven
Boulogne and Folkestone
Boulogne and Dover (ferry and hovercraft services)
Calais and Dover (ferry and hovercraft services)

Airports

The following ports have nearby airports: Cherbourg, Caen, Deauville-Trouville, Le Havre, Le Tréport (Eu), Le Touquet, and Calais. Most of the flights offered are to internal destinations, but it is possible to fly to Gatwick Airport from Caen, Le Havre, and in the summer only from Deauville-Trouville.

Telephone calls

French telephone boxes are straightforward to use. They accept 50 centime, 1 franc and 5 franc coins. In a number of French post offices it is possible to make a call from a telephone box within the building and to pay for the call at the counter when you have finished; useful if you do not have sufficient small change.

To dial the United Kingdom from France pick up the receiver, insert coins to the value of at least 1 franc. First dial 19 (to connect you with the international network), wait for the continuous purr then dial 44 (the country code for the UK), followed by the STD code less the initial zero, and finally the number of the subscriber. The procedure for dialling other foreign countries is the same, but use the appropriate country code which will be listed in the telephone box.

To telephone a subscriber within France is quite simple. There are only two code areas: Paris (1) and the provinces. All numbers consist of 8 figures. To make a call within Paris, or one within the provinces, just dial the eight figure number. To dial a Paris number from the provinces dial 161 then the eight figure number. For a call from Paris to a provincial number dial 16 followed by the eight figure number.

Bicycle hire

Bicycles can be hired in a number of ports. The local tourist information office can tell you where the nearest place to hire a bike is. In some places bicycles are hired out by the railway station.

Car hire

Cars can be hired in many ports, both from well known hire firms such as Hertz, and from small garages. Bear in mind that it is necessary to have an International Driving Licence which can be obtained through the RAC before leaving the UK.

Shopping in France

Public holidays

The following are public holidays in France:
New Year's Day (1st January)
Easter Sunday
Easter Monday
Labour Day (1st May)
Liberation Day (8th May)
Ascension Day
Whit Sunday
Whit Monday
Bastille Day (14th July)
Assumption Day (15th August)
All Saints' Day (1st November)
Remembrance or Armistice Day (11th November)
Christmas Day (25th December)

Opening hours

In the smaller towns the shops often close for an extended lunch break from 1200 to 1400 hours.

Banks

0900–1200 and from 1400–1600 hours. Many banks are closed either on a Saturday or a Monday. They often close early the day before a bank holiday. Closed Sunday.

Post offices

Weekdays 0800–1900 hours. Saturdays 0800–1200 hours. Closed Sundays.

Shops

Food shops: 0700–1830 or 1930 hours, Monday to Saturday. Bakers often open on Sunday morning.
Non-food shops: 0900–1830 or 1930. Closed Sunday, and sometimes all or half-day Monday.

Hypermarkets: 0800–2000, 2100 or even 2200 hours. Closed Sunday.

Shopping
Shopping in France is fun. Most harbours have their specialist bakers, pork butchers etc. In the larger ports you will also find supermarkets (*supermarché*) and hypermarkets. Often the hypermarkets are on the outskirts of town, and may be difficult for the yachtsman to reach. The following are some types of shops:

boulangerie bakers.

pâtisserie cake shop, specialising in cakes, pastries, confectionery. May sell bread as well.

épicerie grocers.

fromagerie specialist cheese shop. May sell other dairy products.

boucherie butchers, sells beef, lamb and poultry.

boucherie chevaline sells horse meat. Often pictures of horses in the shop and as a shop sign.

charcuterie pork butchers. May also sell made-up dishes, including salads and vol-au-vents.

traiteur sells made-up dishes such as cassoulet, couscous, salads, etc.

droguerie sells household items such as detergents, toilet paper, paraffin and methylated spirits.

quincaillerie hardware shop.

pharmacie chemists, indicated by a green cross on a white background.

A typical market scene, close to the harbour at Honfleur.

Money

The French unit of currency is the franc which is divided into 100 centimes. The rate of exchange varies, but as an approximate guide you can reckon on 10 francs to the pound.

French currency can be obtained by exchanging traveller's cheques or banknotes at banks, post of- fices and *bureaux de change*. The best exchange rate is usually given by banks. Note that the rate of commission varies between banks. Alternatively you can cash *Eurocheques* at a bank, or *Postcheques* at post offices. When changing money you will need to present your passport as identification.

Eurocheques are an easy way to obtain foreign currency or to pay for goods or services. You draw funds from your British current account, using special *Eurocheques* issued by your bank. In addition you need a special *Eurocheque* encashment card and your passport. The *Eurocheque* is written out in English in the currency required; the maximum allowed for each one was 1200 francs in 1989 (about £100). Your bank may make a charge for the *Eurocheques* and the encashment card when they are issued, and will charge a commission when the cheque is debited from your account. The foreign bank or shop does not charge you any commission.

Postcheques operate in a similar way, but are issued by the National Girobank, and are cashed at post offices. There is a special *Postcheque* encashment card. Again the amount required is written out in English. The maximum amount (1989) you can cash on any *Postcheque* is also 1200 francs.

Credit cards such as Visa and Access can be used at banks to draw cash, as well as to pay for services. Note that some hypermarkets do not accept credit cards.

Eating out

Eating out in France can be quite an experience, and is often good value for money. The days of cheap meals in France are however long gone.

It is often difficult to choose between restaurants, but one full of locals would be promising. For some it is necessary to book a table in advance.

Making a selection from the menu can be difficult, particularly if your knowledge of French is limited. The easy way out is to opt for a fixed-price menu. Most restaurants offer one or two options which will be displayed on a board outside. These often offer a three or four course meal, sometimes with wine, beer or mineral water included (*boisson compris*), at a reasonable price. If service is included in the price the menu will say *servis compris*. If service is not included you will be expected to leave a tip of 10 to 15%.

Specialities offered by restaurants on the north coast of France are mainly fish dishes, mussels (*moules*), oysters (*huîtres*), and dishes cooked in cream and *Calvados* (apple brandy). Lamb raised on the salt marshes (*mouton de pré-salé*) is another speciality. Normandy is one of the major cheese producing regions of France, and the cheese board at the end of the meal will most likely consist of local produce. Note that the French do not usually eat their cheese with biscuits or bread, but eat it on its own. If you have coffee at the end of the meal it will be strong and black unless you ask for *café au lait*.

Formalities

On departure from Britain British yachts should complete a British customs form giving notice of their intended departure. This form *C1328* is obtainable from customs offices, and many harbour offices and yacht clubs. The form is completed in triplicate before departure, giving details of crew, and the intended time, date and port of departure. The top copy is then posted to the customs office; many harbours have a special posting box for them.

If the voyage is abandoned the rest of form *C1328* is returned to the customs office to which the top copy was sent with 'Voyage Abandoned' written across it.

On return to the United Kingdom the skipper must report arrival to customs, by telephone (usually on Freephone 100 'Customs'), radio or in person. The yacht should be flying the yellow 'Q' flag, as well as its own ensign. Under certain circumstances the yacht will be able to complete the formalities in a simplified manner, and may not even be boarded. If the yacht is not visited by a customs officer within a certain period of time Part 2 of form *C1328* is sent to customs, and the bottom copy kept for your own records.

For full details of the current regulations governing departure from the UK and return refer to H. M. Customs and Excise *Notice 8*, available on request from your local customs office.

The procedure for British yachts visiting France is straightforward. If you have come from another EC country and have nothing to declare you do not need to take any action. You do not even need to fly the yellow 'Q' flag. Your arrival in port will have been noted by the authorities, and in certain harbours where the customs officials are particularly zealous, you will be visited. If you are not on board at the time, a form will be left for you to complete and return to the French customs (*douanes*).

British yachts can spend six months in any year in France, without having to pay import duty. During your stay you are not allowed to charter your yacht, or to use it for any profit or gain.

Documentation

British yachts travelling to France must be registered, and have the registration document on board. Privately owned yachts can either be registered under the full registry procedure, or (if under 24 metres in length) be registered on the Small Ships Register (SSR). The SSR is administered by the Royal Yachting Association, Romsey Road, Eastleigh, Hants SO5 4YA. The yacht must also have third party insurance. Each person on board must have a passport, or a British Visitor's Passport. Only British and other EC nationals do not need a visa.

Duty- and tax-free allowances

Within the EC duty- and tax-free allowances have been standardised, so that the same allowances apply to every visitor to each EC country. Children under the age of 17 do not have an allowance for tobacco or alcohol.

From experience it is better value to buy wines and beers tax-paid in an ordinary shop, rather than buy these duty-free. On the other hand buying spirits duty-free offers better value.

Travelling with animals

The United Kingdom is free of rabies, and to maintain this situation the authorities have strict regulations governing the landing of animals from abroad. Animals cannot be landed from abroad without an import licence and must spend six months in quarantine. This must be arranged in advance before the animals are landed in the UK. People caught smuggling an animal into the United Kingdom face heavy fines, prison sentences, and the destruction of the animal.

Medical treatment

British residents who are taken ill when in France can receive free medical treatment under reciprocal arrangements made between the British and French governments. To obtain free treatment it is necessary to have a *Certificate of Entitlement* (Form *E111*), which is available from your local Social Security office (DHSS). At present you need to apply at least a month before your intended departure. When the *Certificate of Entitlement* is sent to you details on obtaining free treatment are enclosed. You may in addition like to take out private medical insurance.

Supplies

Drinking water *(eau potable)*

It is perfectly safe to drink the water in France, unless the tap has a notice saying *l'eau non potable*. Most marinas have water piped onto their pontoons, but do not always have hosepipes. It is therefore wise and a lot more convenient to carry your own hosepipe on board. The type which rolls up flat into a compact cartridge is ideal.

Fuel

Duty-free fuel is only sold to fishermen in France. Yachtsmen can buy fuel, duty-paid, from any garage or from marina fuel berths. Diesel is called *gasoil*, and petrol is called *essence* or *carburant auto*, although the pump may have *Super* written on it. Yachts are not allowed to use domestic heating oil (*fuel domestique*) as a propellant.

Gas

Camping Gaz is readily available in France. British and French *Camping Gaz* bottles are interchangeable. *Calor Gas* cylinders, however, cannot be changed or easily filled in France. If you use *Calor Gas* on board it is therefore wise to take sufficient gas with you for your holiday needs.

Paraffin

Pétrole, pétrole kerdane, or *pétrole lampant* is expensive in France (about £5·00 per gallon) and is usually sold in plastic bottles holding a litre. You will find it in *drogueries,* supermarkets, and hypermarkets. Methylated spirits (*alcool à brûler*) on the other hand is about half the British price. It can be purchased in the same shops as paraffin.

Electricity

Most marinas and yacht clubs provide electricity, the cost being included in the marina dues. The supply in France is 220 volts, and you will need to equip yourself with a continental two-pin plug. These can be purchased cheaply and easily in France, and also from camping and caravanning shops in the UK.

French marinas

The marinas and yacht clubs on the north coast of France tend to be reasonably inexpensive and offer excellent facilities. On average French marina dues in this area are about 60% of the charges made in Britain. Most marinas have showers, but these tend to be open during daylight hours only, and there is often an extra charge.

Tourist information

With the exception of Le Hourdel all the harbours described in this pilot have tourist information offices. These may be called Syndicat d'Initiative or Office de Tourisme. The staff are helpful, often speak English and can provide you with leaflets describing the town, free maps and tide tables, as well as offer advice on excursions, bicycle hire, bus and train timetables etc.

Entering the French canals

France is crisscrossed by an extensive network of inland waterways which links up with canal systems in Belgium and Germany (and so ultimately with the Netherlands), and with the Atlantic and the Mediterranean. In the area covered by this pilot it is possible to enter the French canal system at Calais, St-Valéry-sur-Somme, and Le Havre. At all these ports it is possible to arrange for your mast to be taken down.

Use of the French waterways is free with the exception of certain sections. For example a small charge is levied for being towed through one of the tunnels on the Canal de St-Quentin.

The maximum dimensions for vessels using the inland waterways vary, depending on the canal in question. Each year some canals or sections of canals are closed for repairs and maintenance. Information on the canal dimensions and the planned closures, called *chômages,* can be obtained from the

French Government Tourist Office, 178 Piccadilly, London, W1V 0AL (☎ 01-499 6911 or 01-491 7622), from March onwards for the coming year.

A useful guide to the French Canals is *Inland Waterways of France,* by David Edwards-May, published by Imray, Laurie, Norie and Wilson.

At Port-en-Bessin visiting yachts are in the town centre.

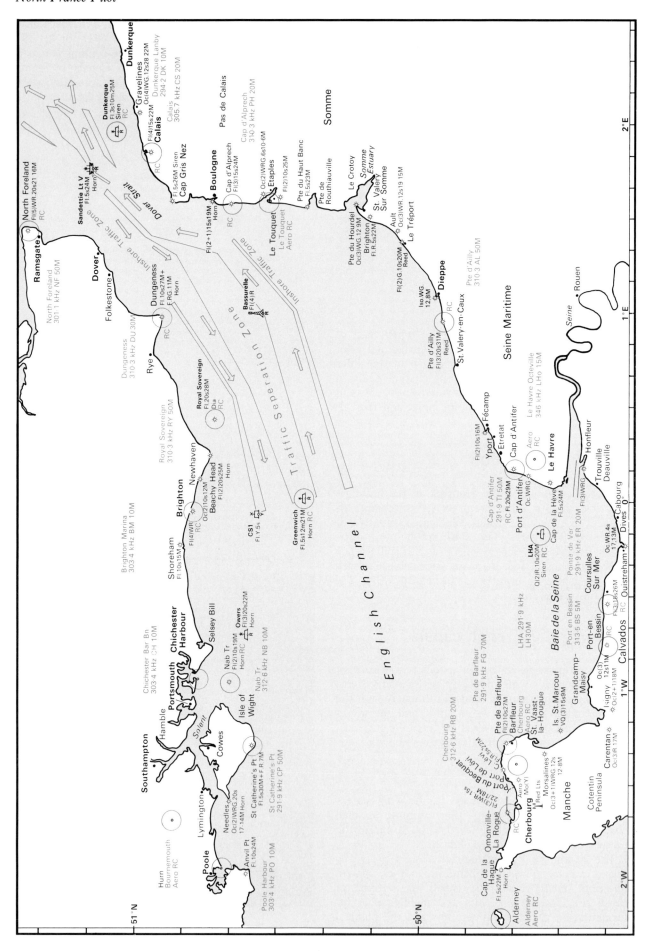

Pilotage

The northern coast of France is described here in an anticlockwise direction, commencing at Cherbourg and working towards Calais. This is the logical way to cruise along this coast, as it takes advantage of the east-flowing flood tide, with the possibility of a favourable wind from the prevailing southwesterly direction. Leaving one port at the earliest opportunity means that you will have the flood tide carrying you eastwards on your way to the next port, where high water will be correspondingly later.

Cherbourg to Barfleur

Charts Admiralty *1106, 2602, 1349*
Imray *C33A, C32*

Cherbourg is situated at the centre of a wide bay on the northern coast of the Cotentin peninsula, a large and roughly oblong-shaped peninsula which projects northwards into the English Channel.

The northern coast of the Cotentin peninsula is an area of strong tides, particularly off the northwest and northeast headlands, Cap de la Hague and Pointe de Barfleur. A mile off Cap de la Hague, for instance, the tide can attain a maximum rate of 6·3 knots on springs, and just over 3 miles off Pointe de Barfleur the tide can reach 5·3 knots on springs. With tidal streams as strong as these it is important to know where you are and what the tide is doing.

The Cotentin peninsula is comparatively low, particularly towards the east, with a shortage of conspicuous features. Consequently it can be difficult to make out from seaward. To compound the problem there are rocky outcrops and shallow areas up to 1 mile offshore to the west of Cherbourg, and almost 2 miles offshore east of Cherbourg.

Cherbourg is a popular first port of call for British yachts crossing from the Solent. It can, after all, be entered in all weather and tide conditions. However, in hazy or misty weather it can be difficult to discern from seaward, and traditionally it has been recommended that yachts should time their arrival for just after dawn. In this way it is possible to obtain an accurate fix from the major navigational lights at Gros du Raz (Cap de la Hague), Fort de l'Ouest (Cherbourg), Cap Lévi and Pointe de Barfleur before approaching too close to the land. There is still a lot to be said for this approach – after all, electronic navigation aids can fail. At night the bright lights at the Atomic Energy Centre at Jobourg, approximately 10 miles to the west of Cherbourg show up long before any of the major navigational lights. Seen for the first time the lights at the Atomic Energy Centre could easily be mistaken for the deck and accommodation lights of a large ship at anchor.

When navigating along this northern coast of the Cotentin it is prudent to keep at least 2 miles offshore in good weather and 4 (or more) miles offshore if the weather is rough. There are tidal races over the uneven rocky banks 2 miles offshore between Cap Lévi and Pointe de Barfleur. The strong tides produce standing waves even in good weather and rough seas in moderate winds if the wind is against the tide. In these conditions it is no place for a small yacht. The infamous Raz de Barfleur (Barfleur Race) lies further east, 3 to 4 miles northeast and east from the Pointe de Barfleur. In wind-against-tide situations, especially on spring tides or in strong winds, the seas break creating dangerous conditions for yachts.

On passage from Cherbourg to Barfleur it is important to get the timing right. You need to take advantage of the strong east-flowing tide, and if heading for Barfleur, need to arrive within 2 hours of high water at Barfleur.

Travelling eastwards from Cherbourg there are three buoys, up to 2½ miles offshore, marking the seaward edge of the rocks and shoals between Cap Lévi and Pointe de Barfleur. Most yachts on passage along this coast hop from one buoy to the next. In poor visibility beware of other yachts working this passage (perhaps with Decca) appearing at close quarters out of the murk.

There is an inshore passage between Cap Lévi and Pointe de Barfleur which is shown on Admiralty chart *1106*, but the transits would be difficult to find, especially with 4 knots of tide under your keel.

When making a passage from Cherbourg to Barfleur keep north of the three buoys, marked *Pierre Noire, Renier*, and *Les Equets*. From *Les Equets* aim to pass ½ mile east of the unlit beacon *La Jamette*, avoiding the Banc de St-Pierre which lies close south of the direct course. *La Jamette* beacon, which can be difficult to make out, marks the seaward end of the drying rocks off Pointe de Barfleur lighthouse. From this point ½ mile east of *La Jamette* steer south, passing to the east of the unlit green buoy marking the rock, *La Grotte*. This course, besides being the shortest route to Barfleur, avoids the race off Pointe de Barfleur.

Cap Lévi lighthouse.

Barfleur to Grandcamp-Maisy

Charts Admiralty *2073, 1349*
    Imray *C32*

The wide, north-facing Baie de la Seine extends from the Cotentin peninsula in the west to the Seine estuary, Le Havre and Cap d'Antifer in the east.

From Pointe de Barfleur SSE towards St-Vaast-la-Hougue drying rocks and shallow areas extend up to 1¾ miles offshore. Some, but not all, of these rocks are marked by beacons.

St-Vaast, guarded by forts on a peninsula and the Ile de Tatihou, is approached from the southeast along a marked channel passing between the island and the peninsula. Dangerous rocks, including La Tourelle which dries, lie up to 6 cables to the east and southeast of the Ile de Tatihou. St-Vaast is famous for its oysters which are cultivated in beds in the bays to the north of Ile de Tatihou and to the southwest of the peninsula. Anchoring in these areas is not allowed.

A 12-mile-long beach, backed by sand dunes, stretches south from St-Vaast to the Baie du Grand Vey. In the northern part the beach is rocky, with rocks extending up to 1½ miles offshore. Towards the southern end, to the north of Pointe de la Madeleine, the beach is fringed by wartime wreckage, dating from the American invasion at 'Utah Beach' in 1944.

Between St-Vaast and Pointe de la Percée (a headland 4¾ miles to the east of Grandcamp-Maisy) a line of shoals and wrecks lies roughly 3 miles offshore, parallel to the coast. Some of these banks and wrecks are dangerous to yachts, and not all of them are marked by buoys. Perhaps the most dangerous wreck lies 2¾ miles northwest of the Iles St-Marcouf – it has barely 0·3m over it and is not marked in any way. In the midst of this line of shoals lie the Iles St-Marcouf. The northern island, the Ile du Large has a fort on it and a major navigation light. From a distance the two islands look like ships at anchor. In the strait between the islands there is an anchorage which makes a pleasant lunchtime stop in settled weather. There is also a small-boat harbour on the western side of the Ile du Large.

In the southwest corner of the Baie de la Seine, at the base of the Cotentin peninsula, is the shallow, drying estuary, the Baie du Grand Vey. Buoyed channels lead across the Baie du Grand Vey to Carentan and Isigny. These channels are liable to shift, and depths may be less than charted. No attempt should be made to cross the Baie du Grand Vey in strong onshore winds. The western side of the Baie du Grand Vey is low and sandy, whilst an extensive drying rocky plateau lies off Grandcamp-Maisy on the eastern side of the estuary. The northern edge of this rocky plateau is marked by three unlit north cardinal buoys. Grandcamp-Maisy can be entered 2 hours either side of high water, in reasonable weather.

Grandcamp-Maisy to Ouistreham

Charts Admiralty *2073, 1821, 1349*
Imray *C32*

Continuing east from Grandcamp-Maisy there are low reddish cliffs to just beyond Pointe de la Percée. In wind against tide conditions a tidal race may be encountered off Pointe de la Percée.

From Pointe de la Percée the coast forms a 4½-mile-long sandy beach. Depths become shallower and rocky ledges extend up to 1 mile offshore. A north cardinal buoy 1 mile offshore marks the approximate position of a wreck. Another two north cardinal buoys mark more obstructions lying inshore which are dangerous to yachts. This beach is another of the Normandy invasion sites, 'Omaha Beach'. The obstructions are the remains of an artificial 'mulberry' harbour.

Again the coast rises to form a long stretch of level cliffs, bordered by a rocky foreshore, which extends nearly as far as Arromanches. Port-en-Bessin lies in a narrow cleft in these cliffs, and can be identified by a signal station on the cliff tops to the west, and an old signal tower 1¾ miles to the east.

5½ miles to the east of Port-en-Bessin is the famous prefabricated 'mulberry' harbour of Arromanches, which was built to assist the invasion of Normandy in 1944. The harbour is referred to as Port Winston in the Admiralty pilot. There are many wrecks and obstructions in the area of Arromanches, but they can all be avoided by keeping 3 miles offshore, north of the most northerly of the three cardinal buoys.

It is possible to anchor within the 'mulberry' harbour at Arromanches, perhaps for lunch, but it offers little real shelter. One would not be tempted to remain here overnight unless the weather were very settled.

The small, unlit red and green buoys which mark the entrance to the 'mulberry' harbour are tucked around the corner and are difficult to see from seaward. Approaching from the west these buoys seem to be on the wrong sides of the entrance. Continue east past the entrance, before changing course to enter, and the true layout of the approach will become apparent. The cleared official anchorage at Arromanches is close to the entrance, and is exposed to wind, swell, and tide.

1½ miles offshore to the northeast of the entrance to the harbour at Arromanches there is a drying rocky shoal, the Rocher du Calvados. From Arromanches 10 miles east towards Ouistreham the rocky coastal bank, the Plateau du Calvados, extends almost 2¾ miles offshore. Much of it dries or is very shallow, and there are several unmarked dangerous wrecks in the area. It is as well to keep at least 2½ miles offshore, or more if the weather is bad. There is a channel across the rocks leading to Courseulles-sur-Mer which can be entered two hours either side of high water. This channel is approached from a lit safe-water buoy, moored approximately 1 mile north of the harbour entrance. Beware of the possibility that this buoy may not be in its charted position. In reasonable weather it is possible to anchor close to the buoy while you await the tide, but swell can make it an uncomfortable anchorage!

Between Courseulles and Ouistreham, about 10 miles away, the Plateau du Calvados extends up to 2¾ miles offshore. An unlit north cardinal buoy, Essarts, lies 9 cables northeast of the shallows at Pointe des Essarts. There are three wrecks in the area marked by unlit cardinal buoys.

Ouistreham lies at the mouth of the river Orne and is where the Canal de Caen enters the sea. Sediment carried down by the river has created a wide sand and shingle bank stretching 2¾ miles offshore. These dangers mean that you have to stay well offshore, and in hazy weather the low-lying coast and estuary can be difficult to see. There is however a tall lighthouse, painted white with a red top, at the entrance to the Canal de Caen, and buoys marking the deep-water dredged channel to the harbour entrance are encountered almost 1½ miles offshore. Submerged training walls, marked by beacons, extend almost 1 mile offshore on both sides of the channel. Beware of strong tidal currents which set across the channel and could carry you into danger. The channel is dredged to 2·6 metres. In strong onshore winds (northwest to northeast) the approach channel is dangerous.

Besides being the point at which seagoing ships enter the Canal de Caen with cargo for the industrial complex north of Caen, Ouistreham is a fishing and ferry port. There is a large and well sheltered marina entered from the ship canal at Ouistreham.

The dangers between Courseulles and Ouistreham (which include the remains of blockships 1 mile offshore) are covered by the red sector of the light at Ouistreham.

Ouistreham to Cap de la Hève

Charts Admiralty *1821, 2146, 1349, 2990*
Imray *C32, C31*

From Ouistreham eastwards the coast continues low and sandy, only rising to the east of the Dives estuary. Shallow depths, including a spoil ground nearly 2½ miles offshore marked on its northern edge by a lit north cardinal buoy, are a feature of this coast.

It is possible to enter the river Dives at high water; there is a fish quay and yacht club at Dives, and a yacht club with pontoons and moorings further upstream at Cabourg. Tidal streams in the Dives estuary are strong, particularly on the flood when the current can reach 5 knots coming round Pointe de Cabourg. The unlit buoys which mark the drying channel can be difficult to locate from seaward, but the wooded hills rising immediately to the east of the Dives estuary aid identification. The cliffs to the northeast of Dives, the Falaises des

Vaches Noires are distinctive, being dark brown in colour and cut by deep gullies. They can best be described as being like spoil tips falling down the cliff face.

The next ports to the northeast of Dives are Deauville and Trouville which share a common entrance at the mouth of the river Touques. Depths off this stretch of coast are again comparatively shallow, and it is as well to be at least 1½ miles offshore in reasonable weather, further off in bad weather. A lit west cardinal buoy, *Trouville SW*, lies 1 mile WNW of the entrance to Deauville-Trouville. The approach to the harbour lies between submerged training walls, marked by beacons and light platforms at the ends. Northeast of the harbour entrance an unlit red buoy, nearly 3 cables offshore, marks the seaward end of a ruined submerged jetty.

The coast from Deauville-Trouville northeastwards is bordered by a rocky bank, extending in places up to 1·2 miles offshore. Depths also become increasingly shallow further offshore, because of silt carried out to sea by the river Seine. The Admiralty pilot advises vessels to stay west of a line drawn between Trouville and Les Ratelets, a sandbank at the mouth of the Seine, on account of the shallow depths. There is in fact no reason to go east of this line, because if you wish to go up to Honfleur you have to first head in a generally northerly direction to enter the Chenal de Rouen.

Sandbanks at the mouth of the Seine dry, and shallow depths extend for some distance offshore, and are constantly changing. Buoys may not be in their charted positions, and caution is necessary. The Banc de Seine, which stretches approximately 15 miles to the west of the estuary, has depths of less than 15 metres over it. Heavy seas can be encountered in this area when the wind is against the tide. Tidal streams can reach 1·8 knots on springs.

There is a heavy concentration of commercial shipping in this area. Large cargo ships enter the Seine bound for Rouen, and other ships, fishing boats, and ferries converge on the port of Le Havre.

A dredged ship channel, the Chenal de Rouen, contained between submerged training walls and marked by beacons, leads into the Seine, and up to Honfleur and beyond. Drying sandbanks have built up along the channel side of the northern training wall, so it is essential to keep an eye on the echo sounder.

Tidal streams in the Seine and approaches are strong – up to 4 knots in places – and complex. It is therefore best to enter on the flood, and depart on the ebb. Ships will be encountered following the same tactics. Incidentally these ships are fast moving, and as they are constrained by their draught, it is essential to keep out of their way.

If you wish to go up the Seine to Rouen this is possible without lowering your mast, but to proceed beyond Rouen masts must be lowered. Timing is critical to ensure that you carry the flood all the way up to Rouen. *A Cruising Guide to the Lower Seine* by E. L. Howells (Imray Laurie Norie & Wilson) is essential reading, giving advice on tides and much else

besides. If conditions at the mouth of the Seine are rough it is possible to enter the Canal de Tancarville from within the dock complex at Le Havre.

Le Havre is one of the major ports of France. It sprawls along the northern bank of the Seine estuary, a mass of storage tanks, towers and factories. Identification is easy, and the buoyed channel leading to the harbour helps in locating the entrance. The tall brown tower of the church of Saint Joseph, lying close to the yacht harbour, the white port signal tower at the entrance, and two tall chimneys with red and white tops are also useful aids. Le Havre is the only haven in this region which is accessible at all states of the tide and in almost all weather conditions.

If approaching Le Havre from a distance the main buoyed ship channel extends well offshore, and there is also a lanby, *LHA*, painted with red and white stripes, in position 49°31'·6N 0°09'·8W just over 10 miles northwest of the harbour entrance. Note also the presence of a platform, *Parfond*, surrounded by cardinal buoys 4½ miles southwest of the *LHA* lanby. Just south of the platform there is a dangerous wreck. Another wreck, marked by a lit north cardinal buoy lies 1¾ miles NNE of the platform. A red and white safe-water light buoy, *HP*, lies 6¾ miles west of Le Havre harbour entrance.

Nearly 2 miles to the northwest of Le Havre entrance there is a major lighthouse at Cap de la Hève, on top of reddish-brown and white cliffs. Note the presence of a shallow bank extending approximately 1 mile southwest of Cap de la Hève.

Cap de la Hève to Le Tréport

Charts Admiralty *2613, 2612, 2147, 1351*
Imray *C31*

From Cap de la Hève north-northeast to Cap d'Antifer and then northeast to Ault, 4 miles northeast of Le Tréport the coast consists of chalk cliffs backed by rolling hills. In the vicinity of Cap de la Hève the cliffs are reddish, but further along the cliffs are a creamy white or grey. This is the Pays de Caux, the land of chalk. Fixing your position along this coast can be difficult because of problems in locating and identifying landmarks. There is deep water along most of this coast except for shallow rocky areas within ½ mile of the cliffs, and a few other shallow banks mentioned below.

The main dangers between Le Havre and Fécamp are a shallow bank extending approximately 1 mile southwest of Cap de la Hève; a wreck 4½ miles west-northwest of Cap de la Hève; and a spoil ground 3 miles northwest of Cap de la Hève. The latter two dangers are marked by light buoys. There is an unmarked wreck with just 1 metre over it approximately 1 mile offshore about 4 miles north of the light at Cap de la Hève. Close inshore there are a few drying rocks and wrecks, but keeping 1½ miles offshore clears all of these.

Port d'Antifer, 10 miles north-northeast of Cap de la Hève, is a large oil terminal used by supertankers. It has a long curved breakwater stretching 1½ miles offshore, and a buoyed approach channel which extends nearly 12 miles offshore. On passage along this coast the Port d'Antifer approach channel may only be crossed west of buoys *A21* and *A22*. Needless to say priority must be given to vessels using the channel. There is a major lighthouse, a grey octagonal tower, on the cliff top at Cap d'Antifer.

Between Cap d'Antifer and St-Valéry-en-Caux there is deep water to within ½ mile of the base of the cliffs. At St-Valéry-en-Caux an area of shallow water extends ¾ mile offshore to the east of the harbour entrance. 6½ miles to the east of St-Valéry, off St-Aubin-sur-Mer and designated on the chart as the Raz de St-Michel, another shallow rocky bank stretches 1 mile offshore. The race is caused by a strong eddy running over this rocky bank. From here northwards and eastwards the seabed becomes increasingly uneven, making the seas considerably rougher in bad weather, with breaking waves in some conditions. The Grands Ecamias and the Petits Ecamias lying 4 miles and 6½ miles respectively north of Pointe d'Ailly are dangerous in rough weather. In addition there are a number wrecks in the area. It is therefore essential to consult the chart.

During April, May and October a firing range between St-Valéry-en-Caux and Veules-les-Roses to the east may be operating. The area of danger extends up to 6½ miles offshore. When firing is taking place a red flag is flown at Fécamp and Dieppe.

At Pointe d'Ailly there is a major light on a square tower painted white which is surrounded by woods. This headland has an area of drying rocks and shallow water up to ½ mile offshore. A dangerous wreck with just 1 metre over it, marked by a lit north cardinal buoy, lies approximately 1½ miles north-northwest of Pointe d'Ailly lighthouse. Another wreck (unmarked) lies 1¾ miles west-northwest of Pointe d'Ailly.

Continuing eastwards from Pointe d'Ailly towards Dieppe keep at least 1 mile offshore to avoid the coastal bank which dries in parts up to 4 cables offshore. Off Dieppe you will need to keep even further offshore to avoid a shallow bank nearly 3 miles long, lying up to 1½ miles offshore and stretching northeastwards from Dieppe.

Two wrecks, one marked by a west cardinal light buoy and the other by an unlit west cardinal buoy lie 6½ miles north and 7½ miles NNE of Dieppe.

Between Dieppe and Le Tréport the coastal bank is shallow, drying in parts, and extending up to ½ mile offshore. Two shallow banks with 4·9 metres (Ridens du Tréport) and 3·1 metres (Banc Franc-Marque) lie approximately 3 miles northwest and 2 miles north of Le Tréport.

Le Tréport to Cap Gris-Nez

Charts Admiralty *2612, 2451, 1892, 438*
Imray *C31*

From Le Tréport onwards the coastal bank becomes wider, and the number of wrecks increases. At Ault the chalk cliffs give way to low-lying land and sand dunes. Sand dunes continue as far as the brown cliff forming Cap d'Alprech, the headland approximately 2½ miles south of the entrance to Boulogne harbour. Between Boulogne and Cap Gris-Nez the foreshore becomes rocky and there are more cliffs.

Parallel to this coast there are a number of shallow banks. These banks – Quemer, Bassurelle de la Somme, Battur, Bassure de Bas and Vergoyer – are dangerous to yachts in strong winds, particularly those from the west. In these conditions the seas break heavily on the banks.

The predominant features of the coast from Ault to Boulogne are the three shallow estuaries of the Baie de la Somme, the Baie de l'Authie, and the river Canche. The estuaries dry, and drying banks extend some distance offshore. Between Baie de la Somme and Baie de l'Authie the shallow coastal bank extends up to 3 miles offshore.

Buoyed channels lead across the estuaries of the Somme, l'Authie and the Canche to small fishing ports. The channels are constantly shifting and the buoyage is changed accordingly. It is however difficult for the harbour authorities to keep up with the changes, so caution is called for. In good weather and visibility, when there is little swell, and at the correct time it is possible to enter the Somme and the Canche. Note however that because of the constantly moving channels and the shallow depths conditions at the entrances to the Somme and Canche can be very dangerous in bad weather. Even in moderate weather entering or leaving the Baie de la Somme, for instance, can be pretty hairy! The Admiralty pilot paints a grim picture of the dangers of stranding when entering the Baie de la Somme. The fine sand can be washed away from beneath a stranded vessel leading to capsize. Having said that the Baie de la Somme has an active yachting community, particularly at St-Valéry-sur-Somme, and is well worth a visit in good weather. The fishing port of Etaples up the Canche is also worth a visit.

The Baie de l'Authie, on the other hand, is treacherous and no attempt should be made to enter. Even the French yachtsmen's almanacs warn against entry. The only vessels which enter it are specially constructed shallow-draught fishing boats. It is as well to keep well clear of the Baie de l'Authie particularly in onshore winds since the flood tide sets strongly into the estuary.

There are distinctive lighthouses close to the entrances of all three estuaries, aiding correct identification. The Somme can be identified by the lighthouses at Brighton (located 1¾ miles NNE of Cayeux-sur-Mer) and Le Hourdel. The Brighton light is a white tower with a red top, whilst the light at Le Hourdel is a white tower with a green top. A

The entrance to Le Tréport, viewed from north.

tall white tower painted with red bands at Berck-Plage on the northern side of the entrance to the Baie de l'Authie stands out well. There are two light structures at the entrance to the Canche. The more conspicuous lies in the resort of Le Touquet and is an orange-red octagonal tower painted with a brown band. The light structure at Camiers on the northern side of the estuary is a metal latticework tower, painted red, and does not show up well.

Note that there is an area west of the Baie de la Somme where anchoring and fishing are prohibited on account of wartime mines. Surface navigation on the other hand is considered to be safe. The extent of this area is shown on the chart.

There are a considerable number of wrecks in this area, calling for close attention to the chart, and care should you need to anchor. The main wrecks to beware of lie close to the approaches to the estuaries. Two drying wrecks lie south-southwest of the lit north cardinal buoy (*ATSO*) off the entrance to the Somme. One is just over 1 mile from the buoy, whilst the other is just under 1 mile from it. Two miles northeast of the *ATSO* buoy is the first of another pair of drying wrecks.

An unlit west cardinal buoy lying 1·2 miles offshore and 2 miles southwest of Pointe de Routhiauville (the headland marking the southern entrance point to the Authie) marks a wreck.

A drying wreck, marked by an unlit west cardinal buoy, is located approximately 2 miles northwest of the lighthouse at Le Touquet. It lies within the white sector of the light at Camiers and is close to the entrance channel to the Canche.

Continuing north from the Canche estuary the coastal bank gradually decreases in extent. Sand dunes give way to the brown cliffs of Cap d'Alprech. The port of Boulogne lies north of Cap d'Alprech. The lighthouse built on the top of the cliff at Cap d'Alprech is like a helter-skelter – the white tower has a staircase spiralling round the outside. Between Cap d'Alprech and the southern breakwater of Boulogne harbour the coast is rocky with a fort built on a drying rock. The hoverport is located in this bay at Le Portel. At night when a hovercraft is expected leading lights are shown at the hoverport.

The port of Boulogne is a major fishing and ferry port, and can be entered at any state of the tide. In clear weather it is easily identified by its size, the cathedral cupola, and the harbour wall. To the north of the town and east of the harbour entrance the Colonne de la Grande Armée is conspicuous. Beware of ferries and other shipping in this area.

The coast between Boulogne and Cap Gris-Nez is rocky with cliffs in places. Drying rocks lie up to 4 cables offshore. There are a number of wrecks between Boulogne and the now disused port of Ambleteuse. A dangerous wreck with masts lies 1¾ miles northwest of Pointe de la Crêche (at the root of Boulogne's northern breakwater). It is marked by a light buoy. 3 miles north-northwest of Pointe de la Crêche there is another wreck (unmarked) with 4·4 metres. One lying approximately 8½ cables southwest of the offlying fort of Ambleteuse dries, and is shown to be on the 10 metre line. Between Boulogne and Ambleteuse the northern part of the shallow bank, the Bassure de Bas, lies approximately 2 miles offshore and runs parallel to the coast.

The headland of Cap Gris-Nez, approximately 9 miles to the north of Boulogne is the closest point to England. The lighthouse, a white tower, stands on the cliffs.

Cap Gris-Nez to Calais

Charts Admiralty *1892, 1352*
Imray *C8, C30*

From Cap Gris-Nez to Cap Blanc-Nez an area of shallow water with less than a metre over it extends in places nearly 1¾ miles offshore. One bank the Banc à la Ligne stretches 3 miles northeast of Cap Gris-Nez. It has depths of less than 1 metre over it, and its position and extent are liable to change. A continuation of this bank, La Barrière, also has depths of less than 1 metre in parts. 4 miles northeast of Cap Gris-Nez and ½ mile offshore lies an area of drying rocks, Les Gardes.

Cap Blanc-Nez, a white cliff on which there is a tall obelisk, the Dover Patrol Monument, is 6 miles to the northeast of Cap Gris-Nez. 1½ miles northwest of Cap Blanc-Nez lies a reef, Les Quenocs, which has just 2·3 metres over it. Overfalls occur to

the north of Les Quenocs. Between Les Quenocs and Cap Blanc-Nez is another area of reefs, Le Rouge Riden. There are a number of wrecks to the west of Cap Blanc-Nez within 1½ miles of the coast.

From Cap Blanc-Nez the coast curves round to Calais. There are chalk cliffs as far as the village of Sangatte. From Sangatte to Calais the coast is low-lying.

The approach to Calais is guarded by two sand-banks, the Ridens de Calais and the Ridens de la Rade. The Ridens de Calais stretch in a line southwest–northeast for approximately 6 miles. The southwest extremity is marked by a lit west cardinal buoy, *CA4*. The Ridens de Calais have a least depth of 7·9 metres over them. In bad weather the seas break on them, and their position may change. The Ridens de la Rade lie between the Ridens de Calais and the shore and have depths of 0·1 metre in places. The approach channel to Calais is entered from the west and is well buoyed. Note however that shallow depths lie close to either side of the channel, and that the buoys marking the shallow area off Bleriot-Plage, 1½ miles to the west of the entrance to Calais are not lit.

Beware of ferries in the approach channel to Calais.

Calais' remarkable neo-Flemish town hall.

Distances in nautical miles

	Omonville	Cherbourg	P. de Becquet	P. de Lévi	Barfleur	St-Vaast	I. St-Marcouf	Carentan	Isigny	Grandcamp	Port-en-Bessin	Arromanches	Courseulles	Ouistreham	Dives	Trouville	Honfleur	Le Havre	Fécamp	St-Valéry-en-Caux	Dieppe	Le Tréport	St-Valéry-sur-Somme	Etaples	Boulogne	Calais
Omonville	0																									
Cherbourg	10	0																								
P. de Becquet	12	5	0																							
P. de Lévi	14	7	4	0																						
Barfleur	25	19	16	15	0																					
St-Vaast	33	27	24	23	10	0																				
I. St-Marcouf	37	31	28	26	13	7	0																			
Carentan	47	41	38	37	26	20	13	0																		
Isigny	48	42	39	38	24	19	11	15	0																	
Grandcamp	45	39	36	35	21	16	8	13	9	0																
Port-en-Bessin	52	46	43	42	28	24	19	24	19	13	0															
Arromanches	56	50	47	46	32	29	23	29	25	15	5	0														
Courseulles	63	57	54	53	39	36	31	37	32	25	15	12	0													
Ouistreham	72	66	63	62	49	45	41	46	42	35	23	18	12	0												
Dives	75	69	66	65	53	49	45	51	46	38	29	19	17	8	0											
Trouville	80	74	71	70	57	54	49	56	52	43	39	35	28	13	7	0										
Honfleur	84	78	75	74	62	57	55	62	58	50	38	34	28	21	17	11	0									
Le Havre	78	72	69	68	55	66	49	56	52	45	33	28	23	18	13	7	10	0								
Fécamp	84	78	75	74	62	65	65	72	68	64	55	48	43	42	39	32	33	23	0							
St-V-en-Caux	96	90	87	86	77	80	80	88	84	80	71	64	59	58	55	48	49	39	16	0						
Dieppe	111	105	102	101	92	95	95	105	101	94	89	80	75	73	67	61	65	55	31	16	0					
Le Tréport	122	116	113	112	104	109	109	120	116	110	98	90	87	100	76	78	68		45	28	15	0				
St-V-sur-Somme	136	130	127	126	120	120	120	132	128	130	122	117	110	110	117	100	100	90	70	58	50	40	0			
Etaples	140	134	131	130	124	130	130	140	136	130	122	117	110	117	100	107	97	75	61	53	43	38	17	0		
Boulogne	143	137	134	133	125	133	133	145	141	135	130	113	118	115	108	104	107	97	75	61	53	43	38	17	0	
Calais	165	159	156	155	147	157	155	170	166	168	162	155	140	138	129	124	127	116	95	81	74	65	63	39	22	0

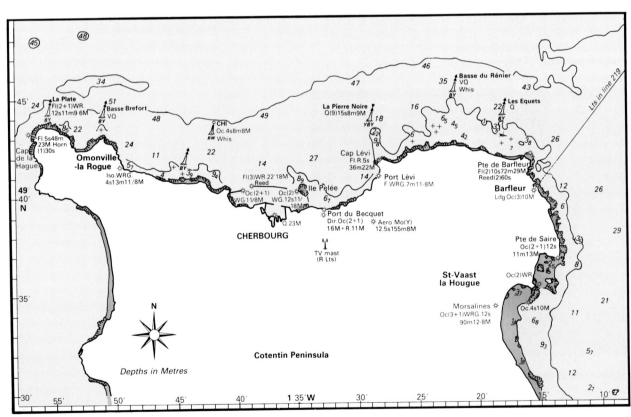

Omonville-la-Rogue

Position 49°42′N 1°50′W
Charts Admiralty *1106, 2669*
　　　　Imray *C32, C10*

General

The small fishing port of Omonville-la-Rogue, surrounded by attractive scenery, lies approximately 7 miles to the west of Cherbourg. It is understandably popular with yachtsmen. In settled weather it is a useful anchorage to wait for a suitable tide before continuing to the Channel Islands. Likewise if you get swept beyond Cherbourg it can come in handy!

In the past Omonville was notorious as the chief port used by Norman pirates. The harbour is strategically located for preying on passing shipping. During the nineteenth century Emperor Napoléon III built a fort here. Today activity in the harbour is restricted to fishermen, yachtsmen, and small boys with fishing lines.

Tidal information

HW approximately Cherbourg −0009 on springs, −0015 on neaps.

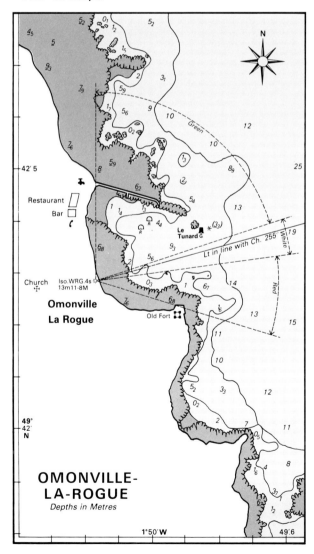

Height of tide above chart datum

MHWS 6·2m, MHWN 4·9m, MLWN 2·6m, MLWS 1·1m

Tidal streams

The tidal streams run at up to 5 knots offshore, decreasing somewhat as the bay is entered. Take care not to be carried off course by the tide.

Minimum depths

The inner part of the harbour dries, but there are 2 to 4m, at least, in the outer part.

Approach

Numerous rocks lie up to 4 cables offshore along the coast to the north of Omonville. The harbour should be approached from the east with the village church in line with the light structure, bearing 258°. At night the white sector of this light leads into the harbour.

An unlit G beacon is situated on a rock, Le Tunard, which marks the extremity of a row of rocks (drying and submerged). These rocks stretch for approximately 1 cable east-southeast from the head of the breakwater. More rocks, including one that is awash, lie up to one cable northeast of the ruined fort. The fort is approximately 2 cables south of the head of the breakwater.

When the beacon marking Le Tunard is abeam alter course onto 285° to enter the harbour.

Lights

Iso.WRG.4s13m11-8M 180°-G-252°-W-262°-R-287°

Berth

The outer half of the breakwater is foul with rocks and it is impossible to lie alongside here. The inner part of the breakwater is used by the local fishing boats. It is best to anchor in the bay, or to pick up one of the buoys laid for visitors.

Shelter

Good shelter from west to southeast. The harbour is exposed to east winds.

Officials

None.

Harbour dues

None.

Facilities

Water tap on the north side of a building near the public toilets, at the head of the harbour wall. Bar and restaurant overlooking the harbour. Telephone. Small grocery store in the village.

To see

The village has a thirteenth-century church. There are some attractive walks in the area, if conditions allow you to leave your boat unattended.

Cherbourg

Position 49°39′N 1°37′W
Charts Admiralty *1106, 2602* (plan), *2613, 2656,*
2669
Imray *C32, C10*

General

Cherbourg is a large commercial, naval, and ferry port, which can be entered at any state of tide and in all weather conditions. A large and sheltered marina caters for the needs of the hundreds of visiting yachtsmen. Although the marina lacks character it has most of the necessary facilities, and is within a reasonable distance of the city, the shops, and restaurants. It is worthwhile spending a few days here, if time allows, to stock up on wine, beer, and other goods, and to explore the city itself. Cherbourg has a lot to offer the visitor besides a berth for the night.

For South Coast yachtsmen based in the Weymouth to Solent area Cherbourg makes a convenient port of entry to France. It also has its advantages as a departure port.

The outer harbour of Cherbourg, the Grande Rade, is protected by massive breakwaters on which there are old forts. Entry to the harbour is through one of two wide entrances, although there is a third entrance close to the shore on the east side.

Beyond the Grande Rade is the Petite Rade. Leading from the west side of the Petite Rade is a series of naval docks. The yacht harbour opens off the south side of the Petite Rade, immediately to the west of the Gare Maritime (the ferry terminal). The fishing harbour lies beyond the yacht harbour.

Tidal information

Standard port.

Height of tide above chart datum
MHWS 6·3m, MHWN 5·0m, MLWN 2·5m, MLWS 1·1m

Tidal streams

In the approaches to Cherbourg the tidal streams run east or west at up to 3 knots on spring tides. The tide flows into one entrance and out of the other, at up to 2 knots, the direction changing with the tide. The flood tide flows east.

The entrance to the marina at Cherbourg. The marina is hidden behind the breakwater to starboard. The yachts are at anchor.

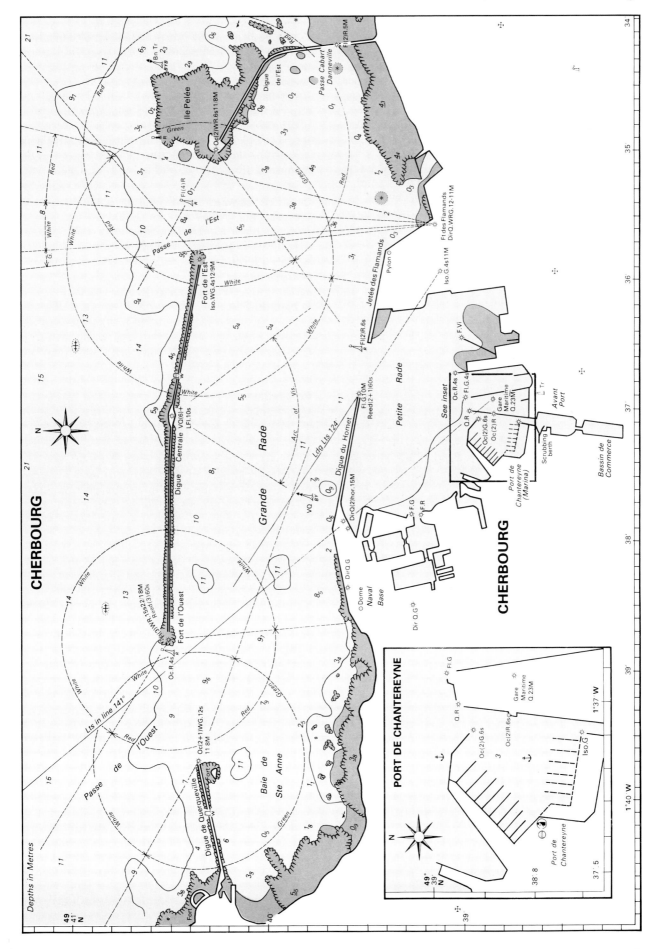

CHERBOURG

Depths in Metres

49
41
N

PORT DE CHANTEREYNE

49°
39'
N

N

1°40'W

1°37'W

38'8

37'5

Port de
Chantereyne

Gare
Maritime
Q.23M

Oc(2)G.6s

Oc(2)R.6s

Q.R

Iso.G

Fl.G

3

CHERBOURG

See inset

Port de
Chantereyne
(Marina)

Gare
Maritime
Q.23M

Avant
Port

Bassin de
Commerce

Scrubbing
berth

Oc.R.4s

Fl.G.4s

Q.R

Oc(2)G.6s

Oc(2)R

F.Vi

Tr

F.G

F.R

Dome

Naval
Base

Dir.Q.G

Dir.Q.G

Dir Q G

Fl.(2)R.6s

Jetée des Flamands

Iso.G.4s11M

Pylon

Ft des Flamands
DirQ.WRG.12·11M

Passe Cabart
Danneville

Fl(2)R.5M

Digue
de l'Est

Passe de l'Est

Fl(4)R

Ile Pelée

Oc(2)WR.6s11·8M

Bn Tr
BYB

Green

Red

Red

Red

White

White

Red

Green

Red

Green

White

White

White

Fort de l'Est
Iso.WG.4s12·9M

Digue Centrale VQ(6)+
LFl.10s

Grande
Rade

Petite
Rade

Fl.G.10M
Reed(2+1)60s

Digue du Hornet

Ldg Lts 124°

DirQ(2)hor.15M

VQ
BY

Dir.Q(2)R

Fort de l'Ouest
Fl(3)WR.15s2·18M
Reed(3)60s

Oc.R.4s

White

Green

Red

Red

White

Lts in line 141°

White

Passe
de
l'Ouest

Baie
de
Ste Anne

Oc(2+1)WG.12s
11·8M

Fort

Fort

Digue de Querqueville

Arc of vis

White

Approach

There is no danger of mistaking Cherbourg in daylight. The city with its tall blocks of flats, factories, port installations and churches is easily distinguished in good visibility. If the visibility is poor the first thing you are likely to see will be the massive harbour walls with their defensive forts. There are water towers and an aerial, shown on the Admiralty chart and in our sketch of the approach, which could be used to fix a position.

There is a landfall buoy 3½ miles north-northwest of the harbour entrance, Passe de l'Ouest, and a west cardinal buoy 2 miles north of Cap Lévi.

At night the most prominent local feature is the nuclear power station about 10 miles west of the city. This shows up long before the navigation or city lights. The first light at Cherbourg to show up is the powerful light on the west end of the central breakwater, Fort de l'Ouest.

The wide west entrance is straightforward, and clear of dangers so long as you keep at least 1 cable away from either fort. They are built on rocky outcrops.

The east entrance is apparently wide, but its eastern half is rocky and shallow. A lit R buoy marks the edge of the deep water. An extensive area of drying rock, the Ile Pelée, lies to the north of the eastern breakwater. Its northern edge is marked by 2 unlit beacons.

At night a sectored leading light assists entry through the east entrance and into the Grande Rade.

There is a narrow and shallow channel through the east breakwater (near its root), which is surrounded by isolated rocks.

The entrance to the inner harbour (Petite Rade) is at the east end of the outer harbour (Grande Rade). On entering the Petite Rade note that part of the east breakwater, the Jetée des Flamands, is submerged. A lit R buoy marks the western end of the submerged breakwater.

The entrance to the marina lies approximately to the south-southwest, immediately to the west of the Gare Maritime.

Lights

Pointe de Barfleur Fl(2)10s72m29M Reed(2)60s RC
Cap Lévi Fl.R.5s36m22M

West entrance

W breakwater Oc(3)WG.12s8m11/8M
   120°-W-290°-G-120°
Central breakwater Fl(3)WR.15s19m22/18M
   122°-W-355°-R-122° Reed(3)60s
Ldg Lts 140·5° & 142·5° Front DirQ.5m15M(2 hor)
   Rear Q.35m23M
R buoy Oc.R

East entrance

Central breakwater Iso.WG.4s19m12/9M
E breakwater Oc(2)WR.6s19m11/8M
Fort des Flamands DirQ.WRG.13m12-11M
   173·5°-G-176°-W-183°-R-193°
R buoy Fl(4)R.12s

Inner harbour

W breakwater F.G.10m10M Reed(2+1)60s
R buoy Fl(2)R.6s

Radiobeacon

Cherbourg *RB* 312·6 kHz 20M Seq 2, 4, 6 Cont
   49°40'·5N 1°38'·9W

Port radio

VHF Ch 9.

Berth

The best berth within this busy harbour is at the marina, to the west of the Gare Maritime. Tie up at pontoon G (the visitors' pontoon), or wherever space allows. The marina has low finger berths, but when it is busy the only space may be rafted up alongside another boat on the end of the pontoon.

It is also possible to anchor to the east of the marina, keeping clear of the channel to the fishing harbour. The bottom is sand and thick weed, and it may take a couple of attempts to get the anchor to set properly. Another anchorage is in the Petite Rade, just beyond the marina breakwater, in 10m at HW. Here the bottom is mud, and the holding good.

If arriving late at night, or if there are strong winds, anchoring is to be recommended.

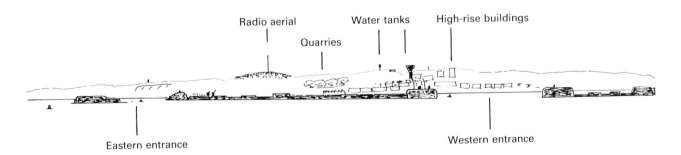

Cherbourg from 2M due north of western entrance.

The fishing boats and official launches tend to set up a large wake when going through this area, and this can lead to damage if you are tied up alongside in the marina.

Shelter

The inner parts of Cherbourg harbour offer good all round shelter. The anchorage in the Petite Rade, however, is rather more exposed

Officials

Harbourmaster and customs in the *Capitainerie* building. Police in the town. British consul, ☎ 33 44 20 13, at the P&O ferry terminal, Gare Maritime. Yacht club. Marina ☎ 33 53 75 16.

Harbour dues

There are marina fees.

Facilities

Water and electricity are laid onto the pontoons. Hot showers are available for a moderate fee at the toilet/shower block near the pontoons and at the *Capitainerie* building from 0900 to 1115 and from 1400 to 1700 hours. Petrol and diesel from the quay near the *Capitainerie*. Close to the marina are duty-free shops, chandlers, sailmakers, chart suppliers, mechanics, telephone kiosks. Travel-hoist, mobile cranes, and a basin where you can dry out alongside the wall (see plan).

Within 10 minutes walk of the marina are banks, post offices, hotels, restaurants, bars, a full range of shops plus all the facilities of a major city and ferry port. Laundrette in Rue au Blé. Market days are Tuesdays, Thursdays and Saturdays (in the square in front of the theatre). On the first Saturday of the month there is a flea market in the Place des Moulins. There is a hypermarket alongside the fish market. Hospital, doctors and dentists.

Cherbourg offers a full range of sporting facilities, including a swimming pool and ice rink close to the marina.

Communications

Ferries to Portsmouth, Southampton, Poole, Weymouth, and Rosslare. Railway station and bus services. Car hire and taxis.

History

When the Romans arrived in this part of France they found a small and ancient fishing village built on the banks of the river Divette where it entered the sea. They must have approved of the site because they built a fortified settlement here, called Coriallum, which continued to be inhabited after the fall of the Roman Empire.

During the latter part of the Dark Ages pirate raids by Vikings, also known as Northmen or Normans, terrorised the northern parts of France. The settlement at Cherbourg would almost certainly have been a frequent target of these raids because of its proximity to the sea. In one Viking raid which took place in AD 841 the church was destroyed.

The Vikings or Normans eventually came to an arrangement with Charles the Simple, king of the Franks, in AD 911. By this treaty the Viking leader, Rollo, acquired the territory which came to be called Normandy.

By the time William the Conqueror had succeeded to the duchy of Normandy the Normans had gained a modicum of respectability and enforced law and order in their territories. In this period of relative peace Cherbourg was able to grow. It was of sufficient size and importance for William the Conqueror to found a new church on the site of the earlier church destroyed by his ancestors.

This church, the basilica dedicated to the Trinity, and much altered over the centuries, overlooks the marina.

During the Middle Ages France and England were frequently at war over possession of the northern parts of France, particularly Normandy. Many towns and villages were attacked, sacked, rebuilt, and changed hands, including Cherbourg.

At one point (1378) Charles the Bad (!), king of Navarre sold Cherbourg to the English in exchange for English help in fighting the French. The English sold Cherbourg back to Charles VI of France in 1404 for 200,000 *livres*. Fourteen years later, after a four month siege, the English recaptured the town and held it until 1450 when Charles VI finally managed to throw the English out of Normandy.

During the fifteenth and sixteenth centuries the people of Cherbourg made a livelihood not only from commerce and fishing but also from piracy, often directed against English vessels.

In 1686 the great military engineer, Vauban, recognising the strategic importance of Cherbourg, drew up plans for extensive new fortifications. Work on the fortifications started, but three years later it was brought to a halt and the fortifications already built were destroyed on the orders of Louvois, Louis XIV's minister of war. Louvois' reason: if the English captured a fortified Cherbourg it would be impossible to dislodge them!

Admiral Tourlaville must have bitterly regretted this decision in 1692 after his defeat by the English navy at the Battle of La Hougue, when he was unable to get any assistance or protection at Cherbourg.

Until the late eighteenth century the harbour was very exposed, but in 1770 work began on constructing the large outer breakwater. The harbour improvements were completed under Napoléon, who boasted that he would recreate the wonders of Egypt at Cherbourg. The huge equestrian statue of Napoléon, gesturing towards the harbour, commemorates this boast.

During the Second World War Cherbourg was occupied and heavily fortified by the Germans. The port defences were so strong that in 1944 the Americans had to attack Cherbourg from the landward side. When the Americans finally reached the port they found that the Germans had systematically destroyed it. It took several months of hard work by the people of Cherbourg and the Allies before the harbour could be used to support the Allied invasion of Europe. In the meantime PLUTO (the pipeline under the ocean) was laid from the Isle of Wight to a point near Cherbourg and brought into operation, supplying fuel for the vehicles of the invasion.

Cherbourg today is a major international and cross-Channel ferry port.

To see

Despite the destruction of the last war sufficient old buildings, including some renovated sixteenth-century town houses, remain to make a walk around the old part of the town interesting.

Near the harbour the basilica dedicated to the Trinity is of interest. The stone columns lining the nave have been painted, something we in post-Reformation Britain are not used to. Above head-height on the north and south sides of the nave finely carved friezes depict the Dance of Death and the Passion of Christ. There are also a number of medieval alabaster plaques, showing religious themes, which were carved in Nottingham and exported to Cherbourg. During the Middle Ages workshops in Nottingham turned out these plaques en masse for the British and European markets.

Above the town the Fort du Roule now houses the museum of the liberation of France. The walk up to the fort is worthwhile, not only for the museum but for the view.

The Musée Thomas-Henry has a collection of paintings and sculptures dating from the sixteenth to nineteenth centuries. The collection includes paintings by Jean-François Millet. There is also a botanical garden and natural history museum at the Parc Botanique Emmanuel-Liais.

On the outskirts of Cherbourg there is a maritime museum at the Port des Flamands, Tourlaville.

About 3 miles outside of Cherbourg is the Renaissance Château de la Tourlaville which is connected with a tragic love story. The strong feelings which existed between brother and sister, Julien and Marguerite de Ravalet, caused their parents some concern. They therefore decided to send Julien away to study. When he returned home four years later the parents were dismayed to find that if anything the feelings between Marguerite and Julien had deepened. Julien was therefore sent away to Paris whilst Marguerite, although still very young, was married to an older man. Her husband treated her so badly that she eventually ran away back home to La Tourlaville, where Julien soon returned. The deserted husband spitefully accused Marguerite and Julien of adultery and incest. Marguerite was so petrified that she would be forced to return to her husband that she ran away again. Julien went in pursuit of her. Eventually they found their way to Paris, where they remained undiscovered for 6 months, until Marguerite's husband located them. They were arrested, tried and condemned to death for incest. Despite pleas by their father to Henry IV for mercy they were both executed in 1603.

It is possible to visit the gardens of the Château de la Tourlaville, but unfortunately the castle itself is not open to visitors. To reach the Château de la Tourlaville catch the bus *Ligne 1* at the Boulevard Schumann and get off at Eglantines.

Port du Becquet

Position 49°39'·5N 1°32'·7W
Charts Admiralty *1106, 2613, 2669*
    Imray *C32, C10*

General

Port du Becquet is a small drying port only 2½ miles east of Cherbourg, which will appeal to the independent minded. A pleasant alternative to following the crowd into Cherbourg.

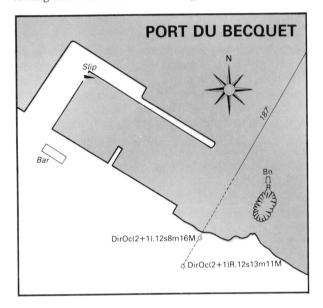

Tidal information

As Cherbourg.

Approach

Port du Becquet is easy to locate once the town and harbour of Cherbourg have been located. The small village lies at the foot of wooded slopes east of Cherbourg harbour. A water tower and aerial behind the village are conspicuous.

Approach from the north, so as to keep clear of the rocks and shallow areas to the east of Cherbourg's eastern breakwater, on a bearing of 187° until the harbour entrance is abeam. Two lit leading marks (white towers) will be seen clearly as you approach. An unlit beacon marks rocks close east of the harbour. Leave this beacon to port and turn west into the harbour. The harbour can be entered within 2 hours of HW.

Lights

Ldg Lts 187° Front DirOc(2+1)12s8m16M
    Rear DirOc(2+1)R.12s13m11M

Berth

Secure bow-to amongst local craft wherever space permits, using a stern anchor.

Shelter

The harbour is exposed to wind and seas from north through northeast to east. It is otherwise well sheltered.

Officials

None.

Facilities

Bar on the quayside. Telephone. Baker and grocery shop in the village.

The tiny drying harbour at Port de Lévi.

Port de Lévi

Position 49°41′N 1°28′W
Charts Admiralty *1106, 2613, 2669*
      Imray *C32, C10*

General

Port de Lévi is a small drying harbour lying on the west side of Cap Lévi, and approximately ½ a mile to the south of the lighthouse. It is used by a few local fishermen, and rarely visited by yachts. In settled weather it is an attractive and quiet place to visit, but lacking in basic facilities such as a water tap. The nearest hamlet lies quite a distance from the harbour.

Approach

The best approach is made from the west where there is clear water. Beware of strong tides in this area. The two harbour breakwaters, which are painted white at their extremities, show up well. A white-painted wall, seen between the breakwater heads, acts as a leading line. The sectored harbour light is situated on this wall.

  Approach and entry are not recommended at night.

Lights

Cap Lévi Fl.R.5s36m22M
Sectored harbour Lt F.WRG.7m11-8M
  050°-G-109°-R-140°-W-184°

Berth

Anchor in 3 to 4m in the bay just off the entrance, taking care to avoid fishing floats and keep boxes. Alternatively anchor in the northern part of the harbour among the local craft, with anchors bow and stern.

Shelter

Sheltered from northeast to south. It is reported that a heavy surf enters the harbour in strong winds from southwest to north.

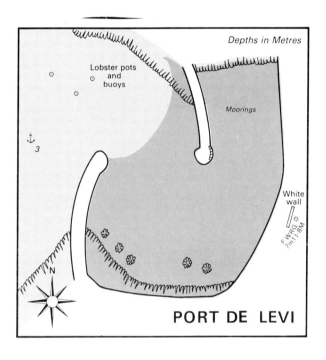

Barfleur

Position 49°40′N 1°15′W
Charts Admiralty *1106, 1349* (plan), *2073, 2613,*
2656
Imray *C32, C10*

General

The historic port of Barfleur is quite unspoilt, although regretfully there is talk of building a marina
here. Yachts dry out alongside, and this is perhaps
why most yachts sail on to St-Vaast, leaving Barfleur to the discerning yachtsman! The rocks in the
entrance are daunting, but the entrance is well
marked and straightforward. Once inside there is
plenty of room, and ashore there are some good restaurants.

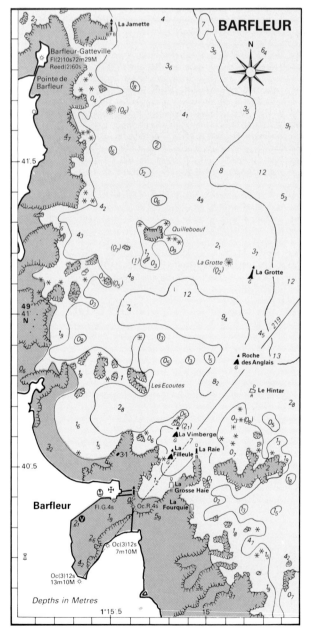

Yachts dried out alongside the quay at Barfleur.

Tidal information

High water is Cherbourg +0058 on springs, +0100
on neaps.

Height of tide above chart datum
MHWS 6·5m, MHWN 5·3m, MLWN 2·5m, MLWS
1·2m

Tidal streams
Tides in the approaches to Barfleur run north and
south, at up to 2 knots. Off Pointe de Barfleur the
current can reach 4 knots. The south-going stream
only lasts for 3½ hours, starting approximately 3
hours before HW Barfleur. If approaching from the
north beware of the tidal race off Pointe de Barfleur
which extends approximately 4 miles offshore, and
which in certain circumstances can be dangerous. It

Barfleur harbour.

should in particular be avoided on spring tides if the wind is against the tide. The race can be avoided by keeping just outside the rocky coastal shoals and the east cardinal beacon which marks the rocks off Pointe de Barfleur.

Minimum depths

The harbour dries completely. There is a good anchorage in the bay just to the north of the harbour where you can await the tide. Take care when entering this bay to avoid the rocks in the approach. Alternatively anchor in the approach channel southwest of the G buoy marking the Roche des Anglais, using an anchor light at night.

Approach

Do not attempt to approach or enter Barfleur in poor visibility. The tall lighthouse on Pointe de Barfleur is distinctive and an excellent aid to locating Barfleur, which lies approximately 1½ miles to the south. The harbour and town are easily identified from seaward. Approaching from north keep to the east of the unlit G buoy marking La Grotte.

Three unlit G buoys mark the east edge of the rocks to the northwest of the channel. An unlit red buoy and two beacons mark the southeast side of this channel. There are also leading marks and lights, but they are not easy to identify in daylight, particularly for the first time. The front daymark is a square white tower built on the southeast shore of the harbour. The rear mark is a white-painted house with a light structure built on its roof, near the most southern part of the harbour. Take care if using these marks not to confuse the front mark with the light on the end of the harbour wall. Once you have identified the leading marks the course is 219°. As the actual entrance is neared the leading marks are obscured, and you can head straight for the harbour. If departing at night steer a compass course until you can see the leading lights.

Off the end of the lifeboat slip there is a G pole beacon. If its concrete base is covered there is a minimum of 1·5m alongside the quay.

Beware of an extra red pole beacon 2 cables east of the entrance, beyond the other beacons. This red pole beacon is not part of the approach channel.

Lights

Pointe de Barfleur Fl(2)10s72m29M Reed(2)60s RC
N Quay Fl.G.4s7M
S breakwater Oc.R.4s7M
Ldg Lts 219° (approximately) Oc(3)12s7/13m10M
  (synchronised)

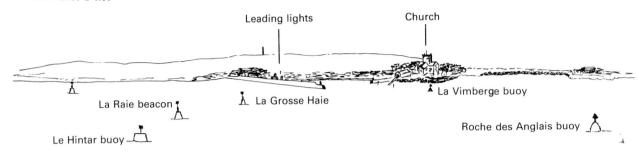

Barfleur, 1¼M off, from northeast.

Saint-Vaast-la-Hougue

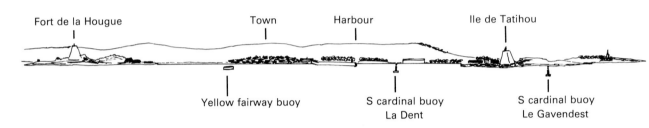

St-Vaast-la-Hougue from southeast, 1½M off.

Barfleur-Gatteville lighthouse from northeast with village and church of Gatteville in the background.

Radiobeacon

Pointe de Barfleur *FG* 291·9 kHz 70M Seq 6 Cont
49°41'·9N 1°15'·9W

Berth

There is a long quay along the northwest side of the
harbour. The yacht berths are alongside the west
end of this quayside, beyond the fishing boats. The
space allocated to yachts is signposted. On arrival
the harbourmaster will most likely direct you to a
berth and will take your lines. There is ample space
reserved for yachts at the inner end of the quay,
where it is safe to dry out. The bottom is firm
shingle covered thinly by mud. In strong north-
easterly winds surge in the harbour can however
cause damage to yachts grounding.

Shelter

In strong east and northeast winds the swell penetrates this harbour making it most uncomfortable.
The anchorage north of the harbour suffers similar-
ly.

Officials

Harbourmaster's office is the small white hut on the
quayside near the church, ☎ 33 54 08 29. Tidal information and weather forecasts are posted here.
The harbourmaster is extremely friendly and helpful. He speaks English (with a Dutch accent!),
Dutch and German.

Harbour dues

Modest harbour dues are charged.

Facilities

Water is available from a standpipe near the quay,
on an adjacent street corner (see plan). The water
laid onto the quay itself is not potable. Public toilet
(dirty!). Fuel has to be carried from a garage. Bank,
post office, a basic selection of shops, restaurants
and bars, pharmacy, marine engineer (M. Boudin,
just beyond the *mairie*).

Communications

Bus service.

History

Barfleur was a Roman and later Viking port. It
reached the height of its prosperity, however, in the
early part of the Middle Ages when Barfleur and St-
Vaast were the most important ports in Normandy.
Royalty used these ports regularly when travelling
between the courts of England and Normandy.

Barfleur, like many other Norman ports, was
deeply involved with William the Conqueror's plans
to invade England. It is said that William set sail
from Barfleur in his ship the *Mora*, a locally built
vessel. The captain of the *Mora*, Etienne, son of
Airard, was a Barfleur seaman. A bronze plaque
showing a typical Viking craft and commemorating
William's departure from Barfleur in 1066 is at-
tached to a rock near the lifeboat slip.

In November 1120 Barfleur's name again appears
in English history books. The only legitimate son of
Henry I of England left Barfleur, accompanied by a
hundred young nobles, in *The White Ship* bound for
England. Unfortunately the ship was wrecked a mile
north of the harbour, on the Quilleboeuf rocks, and
Henry's heir and all his companions drowned. The
only survivor was the butcher, Berold.

In 1196 Richard the Lionheart departed from
Barfleur, with a fleet of a hundred vessels, en route
to be crowned King of England.

During the Hundred Years War Barfleur was em-
broiled in the struggles between the French and the
English, and part of the town was completely
destroyed.

To see

The sturdy seventeenth-century church overlooks
the harbour. It replaces an earlier church, built
nearer to the sea, which was washed away.

It is possible to visit the Gatteville lighthouse at
Pointe de Barfleur on foot. This is said to be
France's tallest lighthouse.

St-Vaast-la-Hougue

Position 49°35'N 1°16'W

Charts Admiralty *2073, 1349* (plan)
   Imray *C32*

General

St-Vaast (pronounced 'St-Vaa') is a popular
destination for British yachts, particularly those not
prepared or able to take the ground. Lock gates
ensure that yachts lie afloat whatever the state of
tide (minimum depth inside is 2·3m). The setting of
the harbour with the forts on La Hougue and the Ile
de Tatihou is picturesque. For gourmets the attraction will be the oysters which are cultivated exten-
sively in this area. They are sold at a number of
shops, and feature on restaurant menus.

Tidal information

Approximate time of HW is Cherbourg +0053 on
springs, +0106 on neaps.

Height of tide above chart datum
MHWS 6·6m, MHWN 5·3m, MLWN 2·3m, MLWS
0·9m

Tidal streams
East of Ile de Tatihou the flood reaches a maximum
of 1 knot on springs and flows in a southerly direction parallel to the coast. The flood starts 5 hours
before HW Le Havre and lasts for 3 hours. On the
ebb it reaches just over 1 knot at springs, flowing in
the opposite direction.

Minimum depths

The approach channel dries out. The marina is dredged to a minimum of 2·3m.

Timing

The lock gates open approximately 2¼ hours before HW and close approximately 3 hours after HW.

Approach

The two forts at St-Vaast make positive identification of the harbour easy. St-Vaast is surrounded by rocky shoals and approach is made from southeast passing between Ile de Tatihou and Fort de la Hougue. The rocks extending from the southeast of Ile de Tatihou are marked by two south cardinal buoys. The rocky ledge extending 5½ cables to the east of Ile de Tatihou is however unmarked. The long promontory southwest of the harbour, Fort de la Hougue, has two east cardinal buoys and an east cardinal beacon marking its offlying rocks. Note that none of these cardinal marks are lit. Midway between these sets of dangers, in the middle of the approach channel is a lit yellow buoy, Fl.Y.2s,

situated in safe water. If you cannot enter the harbour it is possible to anchor northeast of this buoy in 2 to 6m. The bottom is mud with good holding.

When there is sufficient water pass between Ile de Tatihou and the head of the long harbour breakwater. Once past the breakwater you will be able to see the lock building to the west. An inner harbour protects the lock into the large marina. This lock operates from 2¼ hours before HW to 3 hours after HW. A R light indicates that the lock is closed. When it is open a R or G light controls the direction of traffic. As you pass through the lock gates the lock-keeper will tell you (using a piece of card with a letter on it) where you are to berth.

At night the light on Fort de la Hougue in line with the light at Morsalines, 267·5°, leads you just south of the lit yellow buoy and the two south cardinal buoys marking the rocks to the southeast of Ile de Tatihou and into the approach channel. Once abreast of the yellow buoy steer a course to pass to the east of the breakwater.

Note that there are numerous oyster beds north of the harbour, and to the west of Fort de la Hougue.

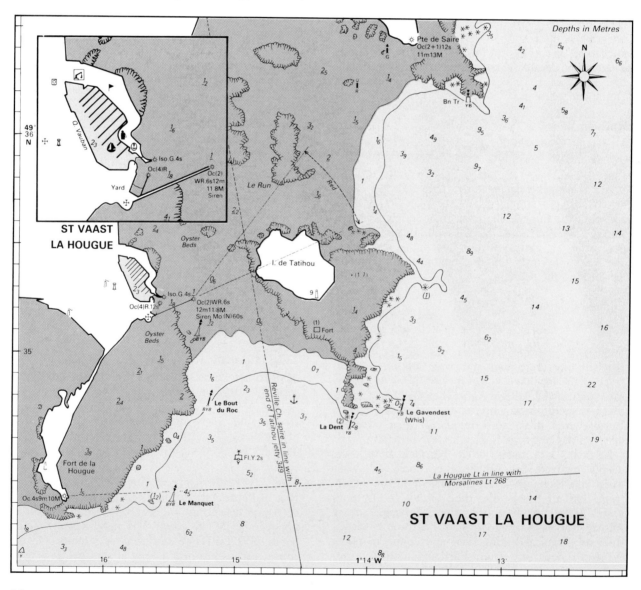

Approaching St-Vaast-la-Hougue with Ile de Tatihou on the bow.

The entrance to the outer harbour of St-Vaast-la-Hougue, with
the lock in the background.

Waiting to enter the marina at St-Vaast-la-Hougue. The marina and lock-operators' office is on the right-hand side of the photograph.

Lights

Pte de Saire Oc(2+1)12s11m13M
Morsalines Oc(3+1)WRG.12s90m12-8M
Fort de la Hougue Oc.4s9m10M
Yellow buoy Fl.Y.2s
Main breakwater Oc(2)WR.6s12m11/8M Siren
  Mo(N)30s
Entrance to inner harbour
  SW side groyne Oc(4)R.12s6m7M
  NE side breakwater Iso.G.4s6m6M

Port radio

VHF Ch 9.

Berth

Berth in the marina as directed by the lock-keeper, whose office is at the lockside. In good weather it is also possible to tie up alongside the outer breakwater, where you will dry out. The quaysides within the harbour are reserved for the fishing fleet.

There is a pleasant anchorage southwest of Ile de Tatihou (sand, good holding) but if you do not want to dry out check your depth carefully. In good weather this is a pleasant place to spend the day, perhaps rowing ashore to explore the Ile de Tatihou, or windsurfing or swimming.

Shelter

The marina provides excellent all round shelter. In strong east and southeast winds there can be a nasty sea in the approaches which makes entry difficult, if not dangerous. The anchorage in the approach is exposed to winds from northeast through southeast to southwest.

Officials

The marina office is adjacent to the lock on your starboard hand as you enter, ☎ 33 54 48 81. Weather reports are posted here. Police in the town. Yacht club with bar in the marina area.

Harbour dues

There are marina dues.

Facilities

Water and electricity are laid onto all the pontoons. Fuel is available from the first pontoon, nearest to the lock. Toilets. Bar at the yacht club. Banks, post office, supermarket, and a reasonable selection of shops. There is a particularly fine *épicerie* (M. Gosselin) in St-Vaast which is more like a delicatessen than a plain grocer's. Saturday mornings there is a traditional market. Hotels, restaurants, and bars. Pharmacy, doctors and dentist. Tourist information. Laundrette in Rue Triquet (near the head of the harbour, see plan). Mobile crane. Repairs to hull (wood and GRP) and engine can be carried out at the traditional yard at the head of the long breakwater. There are also several other mechanics. Charts at the chandlery and at Librairie Madelaine.

Communications

Bus service. Taxis. Car and bicycle hire at Garage de la Hougue, Rue Triquet.

History

With Barfleur, St-Vaast was one of the two most important harbours in Normandy during the Middle Ages, being involved in trade with England and as a departure or arrival point for travellers to the south coast of England.

The town's great claim to fame is that it was off this harbour that the French fleet under Admiral Tourlaville was defeated by the English fleet led by Admiral Russell in 1692. The exiled James II had persuaded the French king, Louis XIV, to help him regain the throne of England. An invasion fleet of barges had been assembled at St-Vaast and part of the French navy was instructed to accompany it across the Channel. Unfortunately for James II the French navy was defeated and the invasion barges burnt before his eyes. He watched the battle and the destruction of his hopes from the church at Quinéville.

The distinctive forts at La Hougue and on Ile de Tatihou were built in 1694 by Vauban, who was responsible for many French harbour fortifications.

St-Vaast claims the honour of being the first French port liberated by the Allies in 1944.

To see

It is possible to land on Ile de Tatihou, either on the beach or at the small drying harbour, and walk to the fort. Like the fort at La Hougue however it is only open to the public on certain days (check with the tourist information office). You can walk across to the fort on La Hougue and wander around it. At the head of the long breakwater there is a simple mariners' chapel, dating from the eleventh century. It is possible to arrange a visit to one of the oyster farms; again details from the tourist information office.

Iles Saint-Marcouf

Position 49°30′N 1°09′W
Charts Admiralty *2073*
   Imray *C32*

General

The two islands of Saint-Marcouf look like ships at anchor when seen from a distance. These fortified islands were inhabited until 1914.

In 1793 a British naval force took advantage of the islands' strategic position to disrupt French naval communications between Cherbourg and Le Havre. Today the southern island, the Ile de Terre, is a bird sanctuary and landing is not normally permitted. Landing on the northern island, the Ile du Large, is however possible. This island, which is the larger of the two, has a navigational light on it, and there is a wrecked fishing boat on the north side of the island.

There are two anchorages off the islands. The better one lies in the channel between the two, closer to the Ile du Large and anchored in 5m (rock and weed). The tide runs strongly through this gap, and swimming from the boat would be dangerous. The anchorage is not particularly well sheltered, and if there is any swell running it will be felt here. In good weather this anchorage is popular with local yachtsmen, fishermen and divers. It is a pleasant lunchtime anchorage whilst on passage along this coast, but is not really suitable as an overnight stop. The other anchorage is just east of the southern island, in 4m.

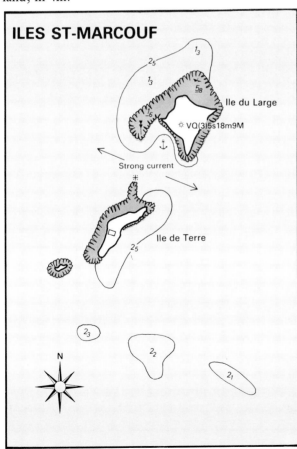

Tidal information

Tidal streams run southeast on the flood and northwest on the ebb. They reach 1·2 knots in both directions on springs. HW is HW Cherbourg +0055 on springs, +0110 on neaps.

Approach

The Iles Saint-Marcouf are situated near enough centrally in a line of comparatively shallow banks which lie parallel to the coast of the Cotentin peninsula. In fresh winds the seas break heavily on these banks. In addition there are a number of wrecks in this area. Perhaps the most dangerous wreck lies approximately 2¾ miles northwest of the islands. It has barely 0·3m over it and is not marked.

The best approach to the Iles Saint-Marcouf is to pass to seaward of the shoals and to enter the strait between the islands from the east. Within the strait there is a south cardinal pole beacon (unlit) lying approximately 1 cable west-southwest of the small harbour on the Ile du Large. Anchor southeast of this beacon in 5m.

A rocky spit extends about 1 cable north from the Ile de Terre.

Lights

Ile du Large VQ(3)5s18m9M

Carentan and Isigny-sur-Mer

Position Carentan 49°18′N 1°14′W
      Isigny-sur-Mer 49°19′N 1°06′W

Charts Admiralty *2073*
   Imray *C32*

General

The small harbours of Carentan and Isigny-sur-Mer lie inland and are approached across the shallow, drying estuary, the Baie du Grand Vey. Carentan lies in the southwestern corner of the estuary, just upstream of the confluence of the rivers Douve and Toute. Isigny lies on the banks of the river l'Aure, upstream of the confluence of the rivers l'Aure and Vire, in the southeastern part of the Baie du Grand Vey.

Of the two ports Carentan offers better facilities for yachtsmen. The former commercial canal basin which had been allowed to silt up, has been developed into a pleasant marina with all mod cons. Yachts lie afloat close to the town centre. Facilities for visiting yachts at Isigny on the other hand are more primitive. The town harbour, if one can use such a grand word for it, is used by a few fishing boats and local yachts which can take the ground. The banks of the river l'Aure are quayed for about a third of a mile, and this constitutes the harbour. There is a pontoon for the use of yachts. Isigny is famous for its dairy products, mussels and oysters, and prides itself on its restaurants.

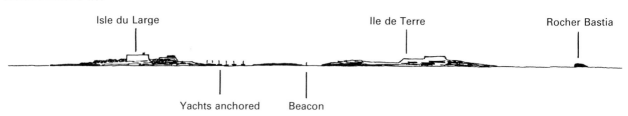

Iles St-Marcouf from northwest, 2M off.

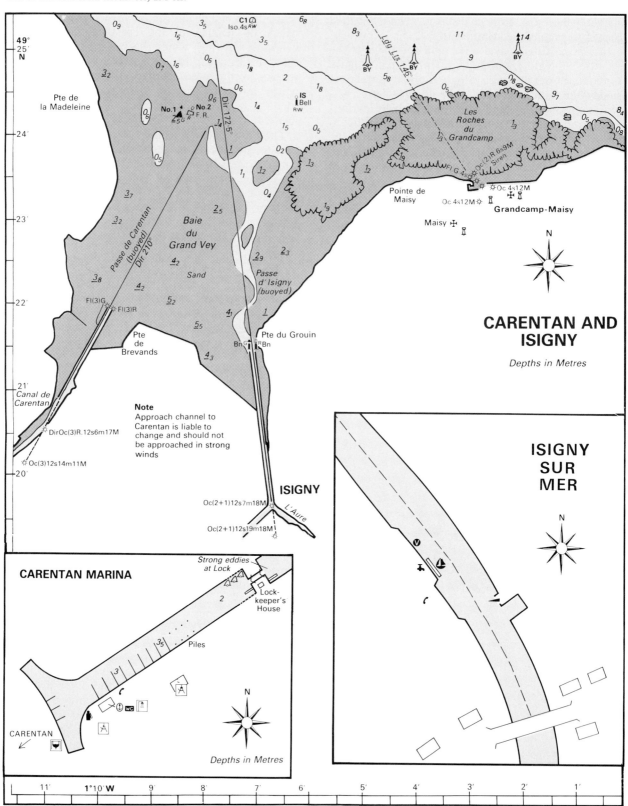

Carentan marina, looking towards the lock.

Tidal information

There is normally sufficient water in the channels across the Baie du Grand Vey for yachts drawing up to 1·5m to navigate 2 hours either side of HW, even on neaps. The tidal streams in the channels are strong, so it is best to time arrival at Carentan and Isigny for HW. At Carentan it is noticeable that the strength of the in-flowing tide is greatest at the lock entrance, where the current can reach 2 knots.

HW at the *C1* buoy, in the approach to the Baie du Grand Vey is HW Cherbourg +0055 on springs, +0108 on neaps.

Height of tide above chart datum
Carentan
MHWS 4·1m, MHWN 2·1m
Isigny-sur-Mer
MHWS 4·2m, MHWN 2·2m

Minimum depths
The approach channels to Carentan and Isigny dry, and the harbour at Isigny dries. At Carentan there is a minimum clearance over the lock sill of 1·8m on neaps.

Timing
The Baie du Grand Vey should only be crossed 2 hours either side of HW. The Carentan lock opens on demand from 2 hours before HW to 3 hours after HW. If possible it is best to time your arrival at Carentan or Isigny for HW, allowing sufficient time to cover the distance from the *C1* buoy to the harbour.

Approach

The land around the Baie du Grand Vey is low and generally featureless, and it can be difficult locating the *C1* buoy at the entrance to the estuary. The estuary itself is shallow and most of it dries. It is very dangerous in strong onshore winds, and in these conditions should be given a wide berth.

The main dangers in the approaches to the Baie du Grand Vey are the unmarked, drying wrecks up to 2 miles north and northwest of the Pointe de la Madeleine, and the rocky plateau off Grandcamp-Maisy. This rocky plateau, the Roches de Grandcamp, extends over a mile offshore on the northeastern shores of the estuary. These rocks are marked on their northern edge by three unlit north cardinal buoys.

Before attempting to enter the Baie du Grand Vey it is important to locate and identify the lit RW safe-water buoy, *C1*. This is moored in position 49°25'·5N 1°07'W. From this buoy you should be able to see the first buoys marking the channels leading to Carentan and Isigny. These channels are liable to change direction and depth, so it is essential to proceed with caution, and to only approach in good conditions. Some of the channel markers are lit, but entry and departure at night are not recommended.

Approach to Carentan

The first two buoys marking the channel to Carentan lie approximately southwest of the *C1* buoy, and are lit. Most of the subsequent buoys are unlit. The final part of the channel leading up to the river mouth lies between training walls, marked on their outer ends by light beacons. Leading lights, 210°, guide you up the first straight section of the river, but they do not help you find the buoyed channel. There are no lights marking the channel upriver, only perches along the river banks.

The lock at the entrance to the marina is located at the confluence of the rivers Toute and Douve. In anything other than slack water there are strong currents, eddies, and even standing waves at the entrance to the lock. It is therefore best to time your arrival for HW or just after. If departing from Carentan 2 hours before HW there is considerable turbulence just outside the lock.

If you have to wait to lock in there is a low waiting pontoon on the port-hand side by the lock. A R light at the lock indicates that the lock gates are closed; a G light indicates that they are open.

If there is no sign of the lock-keeper in the control tower, and assuming that it is within the lock operating hours, moor alongside the waiting pontoon and ring the bell on the control tower for attention. Once inside the lock there are ropes to hold onto whilst the lock is filling or emptying.

Lights

C1 buoy Iso.4s
Ldg Lts 210° Front DirOc(3)R.12s6m17M
    Rear DirOc(3)12s14m11M

Port radio

VHF Ch 9 (Carentan only).

Approach to Isigny-sur-Mer

The first buoys marking the approach channel to Isigny are positioned approximately southeast of the *C1* buoy. The channel, although generally deeper than the channel to Carentan, is liable to change. It is marked by buoys which are moved as necessary. The final part of the channel is straight, 1¾ miles long, and passes between training walls. Leading lights, in line on 172·5°, guide vessels up the straight section of the channel.

At the confluence of the rivers Vire and l'Aure the channel forks to port up the river l'Aure. The harbour of Isigny lies in the river l'Aure, which is quayed for much of its length up to the low road bridge which crosses the head of the harbour.

Lights

C1 buoy Iso.4s
Ldg Lts 172·5° Front DirOc(2+1)12s7m18M
   Rear DirOc(2+1)12s19m18M

Berths

Carentan

When you pass through the lock the lock-keeper will tell you at which pontoon you should berth. The finger berths are low, so arrange your fenders accordingly.

Isigny

There are two possible berths at Isigny, both of which dry out. The better berth is alongside the pontoon on the west side of the river which you come to soon after entering the river l'Aure. The bottom here is soft level mud, although approximately 4 boat-widths out from the pontoon the mud drops away steeply. This berth is a short distance from the town, but is quiet. Drinking water is nearby, and the soft mud bottom is level. Alternatively you can berth alongside the quay, upstream of the pontoon. The mud bottom alongside the quays, however, slopes steeply and there are numerous holes left by the fishing boats. Mooring alongside the quay is not recommended.

Shelter

Good all-round shelter within the marina and at the harbour at Isigny.

Officials

Carentan marina office carries out all formalities, ☎ 33 42 24 44. Isigny marina is administered by the town hall (*mairie*). Yacht club at Carentan. Police in both Carentan and Isigny.

The best berth for a visiting yacht at Isigny-sur-Mer is alongside the pontoon on the starboard-hand side of the channel as you enter the harbour.

The quaysides close to the centre of the town at Isigny-sur-Mer are used by fishing boats. This berth is not recommended for yachts on account of the steeply sloping bottom and holes made by fishing boats.

Harbour dues

The marina fees at Carentan are modest, and as they include the cost of showers and electricity represent particularly good value. At Isigny harbour dues are levied by the town hall.

Facilities

Carentan

Water and electricity to all pontoons. Fuel from the fuel berth. The marina has excellent showers, toilets, and a bar. Chandleries close to the marina. Repairs to hull, engine, sails, and electronics are possible. Slipway, travel-hoist and crane. Swimming pool. Carentan has good shopping facilities, including supermarkets, as well as banks, a post office, laundry (but no laundrette), tourist information office and restaurants. Doctors, dentists, pharmacies, hospital.

Isigny

Water and electricity are laid onto the quay above the pontoon berths. Fuel from a garage in the town, some distance away. Banks, post office, a reasonable selection of shops, restaurants and hotels. The staff in the small tourist information office are very helpful. Doctors and dentists.

Communications

Carentan is served by a railway (main line to Paris and Bayeux). Both towns have bus services and taxis. Care hire at Carentan.

History

The medieval market town of Carentan, set among the former marshes, was known as the 'Capital of the eel'. More recently, since the draining of much of the marsh, it has become an important beef-rearing area. The famous cattle market is held on Mondays.

During the Second World War, American forces landed just 7 miles north of the town at 'Utah Beach', where there is today a monument and museum.

To see

The tall slender spire of the church of Notre-Dame at Carentan is visible for miles across the flat landscape and dominates the town. The outside of the church with its carved statues, and the old houses nearby, are attractive. Unfortunately the interior of the church does not match up to the promise of the exterior. Henry I of England once celebrated Easter in this church.

Carentan prides itself on some medieval arches with houses built above, where a market used to be held.

Carentan is an excellent base for sightseeing. The boat can be left in complete safety at the marina, whilst you go by train, bus or even hire car to Bayeux, Sainte Marie du Mont, 'Utah Beach', or Valognes.

Grandcamp-Maisy

Position 49°23'N 1°03'W
Charts Admiralty *2073*
Imray *C32*

General

Grandcamp-Maisy is an unpretentious little harbour which happily accommodates both fishing boats and yachts. Local and visiting yachts tie up on two long pontoons, whilst the fishing boats berth alongside the quays. The small town seems popular with holidaymakers for whom the usual facilities of popcorn, shooting galleries and other attractions of the fair are provided. Most of the noise, for a change, is not immediately on the quayside! The harbour is popular with visiting yachts. For those with youngsters on board the shrimp fishing amongst the rock pools at low water is said to be very good.

Tidal information

HW Le Havre approximately −0045, HW Cherbourg +0055 on springs, +0108 on neaps.

Height of tide above chart datum
MHWS 7·2m, MHWN 6·0m, MLWN 2·7m, MLWS 1·1m

Tidal streams

In the approaches to Grandcamp-Maisy on spring tides the tidal streams run east at up to 1·1 knots on the flood, and west at up to 1·2 knots on the ebb.

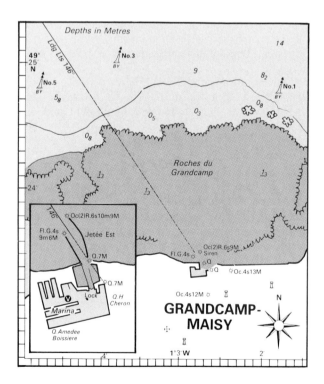

Minimum depths
The harbour is suitable for vessels drawing up to 2·2m.

Timing
The lock gates are open from approximately 2½ hours before HW to 2½ hours after HW. As it happens the lock-keepers refer to the Dunkerque tide tables, opening the gates at LW Dunkerque and closing them at HW Dunkerque. Since it is not possible to moor in the outer harbour, arrival should be timed to coincide with the period that the lock gates are open.

Approach

Grandcamp-Maisy is the first settlement of any size east of the low-lying Baie du Grand Vey, and west of the low even cliffs extending from near Arromanches. The most distinctive features of the town are a church tower to the east, a water tower behind the harbour entrance, and a prominent lattice-type church spire to the west. This harbour should not be approached in strong onshore winds.

A drying rocky plateau lies in the approach to Grandcamp-Maisy and extends over a mile offshore. The seaward edge of this plateau is marked by three unlit north cardinal buoys. Once you have located the buoys you should be able to see the harbour entrance. From a position midway between the west and central buoys the course to steer for the entrance is 146°. Beware of lobster pots set in the approaches.

A short distance off the eastern breakwater an unlit pole beacon marks the end of a rocky spur. On the other side of the channel an isolated light structure marks the extremity of a submerged line of rocks stretching from the head of the western breakwater. Between the breakwaters a shingle bank has built up on the western side of the channel. As you enter beware of a strong tidal set across the entrance.

The lock gates lie ahead, beyond the wave breaks either side. Once through the lock the yacht berths lie to starboard.

Lights

Phare de la Maresquerie Oc.4s28m12M
Phare du Perré Oc.4s8m13M
E breakwater Oc(2)R.6s10m9M Siren Mo(N)30s
W breakwater Fl.G.4s9m6M
Ldg Lts 146° Front and rear Q.4m7M (in unison)

Port radio

VHF Ch 9.

Berth

There are visitors' berths on the end of the more northern pontoon, but in the season space may be limited. You may therefore have to raft up alongside another yacht.

The entrance to Grandcamp-Maisy at low water, viewed from north. Note the unlit pole beacon off the eastern breakwater.

Leaving Grandcamp-Maisy shortly after dawn.

Shelter

Once the lock gates are shut the harbour is well sheltered, but if there is a strong wind with any north in it an uncomfortable surge enters the harbour whilst the lock gates are open.

Officials

Harbourmaster's office, ☎ 31 22 63 16. Police in the town. Yacht club.

Harbour dues

An official comes round the boats early in the morning to collect harbour dues, which are reasonable.

Facilities

Water and electricity are laid onto the pontoons. Fuel is not easily available in the town. The nearest garage is some 2 miles away. Showers (small fee) and toilets on the west end of the fish market building. Weather forecasts are posted up here, at the harbourmaster's office. *Camping Gaz* at a nearby ironmongers. Bank, post office, and a basic selection of shops. There are two chandleries and a laundry/dry cleaners near the pontoons. Several restaurants . On Saturday mornings a fish, fruit and vegetable market is held on the quayside. Tourist information office.

Communications

Bus service (it is possible to catch a bus to Bayeux from Grandcamp-Maisy). Taxis.

To see

This is very much a family holiday resort, with a funfair on the seafront, pleasant walks along the seafront, and a sandy beach with rock pools at low tide.

Port-en-Bessin

Position 49°21′N 0°45′W
Charts Admiralty *2073*
      Imray *C32*

General

Port-en-Bessin is a busy fishing port with smells and oily water to match. Local pleasure craft are moored on drying moorings in the outer harbour. The inner basin, where you can lie afloat against the quay, enjoys all the advantages and disadvantages of being close to the shops, bars and restaurants.

On summer Sundays the scene is particularly lively with a market on the quayside which attracts people from the surrounding districts. As you would expect fresh fruit and vegetables are in evidence. Thick Normandy cream is ladled out of buckets by farmers' wives who also sell their own cheese and butter. There are stalls specialising in oak-smoked hams. Other stalls sell fresh poultry, fish or meat. You will also find craftsmen's furniture, and clothes as well as all the knickknacks of a fair.

Tidal information

HW Le Havre −0043 on springs, −0039 on neaps.

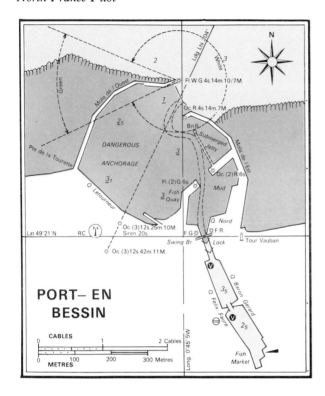

PORT– EN BESSIN

CABLES

0   1   2 Cables

0   100   200   300 Metres

METRES

Height of tide above chart datum

MHWS 7·2m, MHWN 6·0m, MLWN 2·7m, MLWS 1·1m

Tidal streams

Tidal streams run parallel to the coast at up to 1·3 knots on spring tides. The W-going stream starts at HW Le Havre −0300, and continues for 5 hours. The E-going stream starts 2 hours after HW Le Havre and flows until 5 hours before HW Le Havre. When the tide is flowing east there is a west-going eddy of not more than 1 knot just off the head of the eastern breakwater.

The outer harbour at Port-en Bessin seen at high water. Yachts can tie up where the fishing boats are, but drying out in this position at low water is not to be recommended, due to the smell of rotting fish.

Minimum depths

Vessels drawing up to 2·6m can use the inner harbour on neaps. The outer harbour dries completely on springs. The wall on the western jetty in the outer harbour where fishing boats and the occasional yacht tie up to await the tide dries out on all but neap tides.

Timing

The lock gates open 2 hours either side of HW. The swing bridge opens for 5 minutes when the lock gates first open, and then for 5 minutes on the hour. 5 minutes before the lock finally closes the swing bridge is opened again. Outside of these times the bridge opens for fishing boats, and of course, you can follow them through. It is possible to approach the fish quay in the outer harbour 3 hours either side of HW.

Approach

Port-en-Bessin lies in a cleft in the chalk cliffs. It is easily identified from seaward by the semaphore station on the cliffs just west of the town. There is also a disused semaphore tower on the cliffs 2 miles east of the town.

A drying rocky bank extends ¼ mile offshore on either side of Port-en-Bessin. The outer harbour entrance can be approached when there is sufficient water, but not before half tide. It is possible to anchor off the harbour entrance in 3 to 5m (mud, good holding) although it will be uncomfortable unless the sea is calm. Once inside the outer harbour steer into the eastern half of the harbour, passing between two inner walls. Note that a submerged training wall extends roughly north-northwest from the eastern jetty. A narrow canal leads under a swing bridge and through the lock gates into the inner basin. Take great care if entering the inner basin shortly after the gates have opened. There is a vicious eddy just inside the basin which can set you into the yachts moored along the quay. Nearer HW this eddy is negligible.

At night two leading lights lead into the outer harbour on a course of 204°.

The harbour should not be approached in strong winds from northwest, north and northeast since surf breaks within the outer harbour in these conditions, making entry dangerous.

Lights

W breakwater Fl.WG.4s14m10/7M

E breakwater Oc.R.4s14m7M

Ldg Lts 204° Front Oc(3)12s25m10M Siren 20s
    Rear Oc(3)12s42m11M (RC)

Radiobeacon

Port-en-Bessin Rear Lt *BS* 313·5kHz 5M Cont
    49°21′N 0°45′·6W

Port radio

VHF Ch 18.

The inner harbour of Port-en-Bessin viewed from the harbour mouth.

Berth

The best berth is within the inner basin, tied up alongside the west quay near the lock gate. While waiting for the lock gates to open it is possible to tie up on the east side of the fish quay, lying to starboard, which divides the outer harbour into two sections. This berth dries on spring tides and is often used by fishing boats, so it is a dirty and smelly berth at LW.

It is also possible, but only in settled weather, to dry out on the sandy beach to the west of this quay. It must be emphasised that this is dangerous in anything but good weather.

Shelter

The inner basins are well sheltered.

Officials

Harbourmaster and customs are located in the fishmarket building at the far end of the inner basin; harbourmaster ☎ 31 21 70 49. The lock-keeper can also give advice if required. Weather forecasts and other navigational information reports are posted at the lock-keeper's office. Police station in the town.

Harbour dues

Harbour dues are not levied for short stays.

Facilities

Water is laid onto the quays, but a standpipe is required. There is a water tap on the wall of the lock-keeper's office. Fuel is available from a garage on the outskirts of town. *Camping Gaz* from the ironmongers in the town. Reasonable selection of shops. Bank, post office, Sunday market. Pharmacy, doctor. Hotels and restaurants. Tourist information. Fishermen's chandlery. Marine electronics can be repaired. Repairs to wood, steel and GRP hulls can be carried out at the yards at the far end of the inner basin. Mobile crane. Mechanical repairs.

Communications

Bus service (coastal service and to Bayeux). Taxis.

History

This port takes its name from the region, the Bessin, for which it was the main harbour. Bayeux, the capital of the Bessin, is within easy reach. Ancient rivalry with the wealthy merchants of Caen stifled the development of the harbour until the late nineteenth century. A tower on the eastern edge of the town is all that remains of Vauban's seventeenth-century fortifications. The port was captured by British commandos on the 7th June 1944, and swiftly converted into a petrol depot to fuel the Allied advance into France.

To see

Vauban's tower, and the lively Sunday market are worth a closer look. At low tide *pêche à pied* or 'fishing on foot' for whelks and shrimps is a popular local pastime. There is a nature reserve along the cliff tops to the east of the port.

The drying outer harbour at Port-en-Bessin, with Vauban's tower in the foreground.

Arromanches

Position 49°21′N 0°37′W
Charts Admiralty *2073*
        Imray *C32*
        Navicarte *527*

General

The remains of the wartime 'mulberry' harbour (Port Winston) at Arromanches are still impressive, and in settled weather well worth a visit. Photographs, postcards, and reports in history books do not prepare you for the sheer magnitude of the harbour works, and the audacity of the concept.

Although the harbour no longer offers much shelter to a yacht, a visit to Arromanches, perhaps as a lunchtime stop, is a must when cruising along this coast. If the weather is inclement it would however be wiser to make the visit by bus or hire car from one of the nearby ports.

Tidal information

The approximate time of HW at Arromanches is HW Le Havre −0044 on springs and Le Havre −0036 on neaps.

Height of tide above chart datum
MHWS 7·5m, MHWN 6·1m, MLWN 2·8m, MLWS 1·2m

Tidal streams
Tidal streams run parallel to the coast and at up to 1·2 knots on springs. They run strongly, perhaps at up to 1 knot, through the harbour. This is particularly noticeable towards the entrance.

Minimum depths
Although the recommended anchorage near the entrance has 6m at LW, more shelter can be obtained by anchoring closer to the beach in 2m at LW, taking care to avoid an isolated drying rock off the beach.

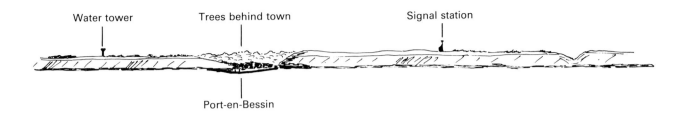

Port-en-Bessin from 3M NW.

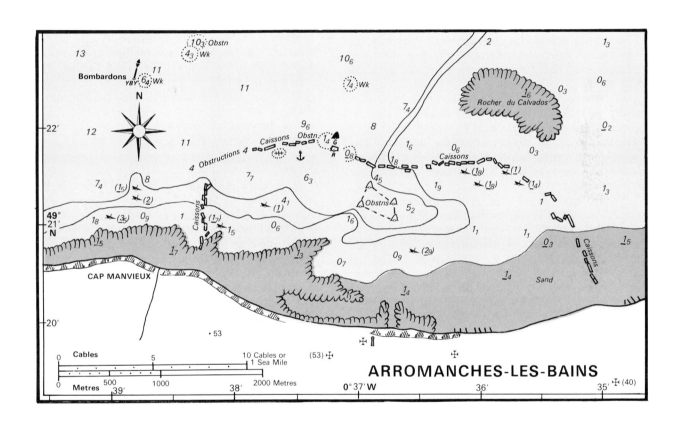

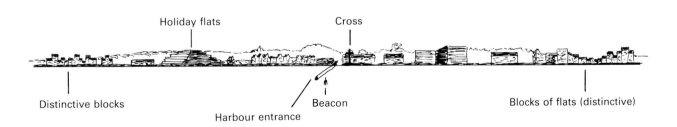

Courseulles from the safe-water buoy.

Entering the ruined wartime 'mulberry' harbour at Arromanches (also called Port Winston). In settled weather this makes an interesting lunchtime anchorage.

Approach

Cliffs either side of the small village at Arromanches are visible from some distance off, and the large caissons are clearly recognisable, particularly as the tide drops.

The harbour is situated on the west edge of a rocky plateau, the Plateau du Calvados. Two east cardinal and one west cardinal buoys (all unlit) mark wrecks north and northwest of the harbour. The middle of the three buoys marks a wreck which only has 0·3m over it at LW. These buoys help to locate the entrance.

The entrance lies 1 mile south-southwest of this central buoy and is marked by two unlit buoys (port and starboard). These small buoys are not easily seen until quite close to the entrance since they are masked from northwest by the caissons. Once the buoyed entrance is found, pass between the buoys on a west-southwest course, giving the submerged obstructions marked by the buoys a wide berth.

Lights

There are no navigational lights. It is therefore inadvisable to attempt to enter or leave after dark.

Berth

Anchor south of the entrance in 6m at LW, or further inshore in 2m. The western half of the harbour has mainly been cleared of wreckage, but 4 white buoys southeast of the entrance mark an area of obstructions. Note also that there is a rocky outcrop drying 0·3m close to the beach. You may feel happier buoying your anchor.

Shelter

There is little shelter. The ruined *caissons* offer minimal shelter from swell and winds. You are in effect anchoring off an open beach.

Facilities

The village of Arromanches attracts numerous tourists to its famous museum of the landings; the few shops cater mainly for the needs of the passing tourists.

History

In June 1944 the small and unremarkable village of Arromanches entered the history books. The village was chosen as the location of one of the artificial harbours, called 'mulberry' harbours, which were to provide backup support for the invasion of Normandy.

The Allied leaders realised that the initial invasion troops would be driven back into the sea unless they could be reinforced by further troops and supplies. Such supplies would have to come in by sea, and it was unlikely that Allied troops would be able to capture one of the major ports within the first few days of the invasion. Winston Churchill came up with the audacious concept of building a harbour in kit form in Britain and towing it across to the French coast. Once in position the 146 concrete barges, or caissons, were to be sunk, so forming the harbour walls.

There were two 'mulberry' harbours, one at Arromanches and one to the west of Port-en-Bessin, opposite Colleville-sur-Mer. The latter harbour however was destroyed in a violent storm on 19th June 1944. The wrecked caissons are marked on the chart.

The harbour of Arromanches was vital to the ultimate success of the invasion of Normandy.

To see

The modern museum overlooking the beach at Arromanches attracts thousands of visitors, and if you do not mind queuing is worth visiting. There is a splendid view over the harbour from the viewpoint up on the cliffs to the east of the village. It is quite a long walk, but once at the top the whole harbour is spread in front of you. During the season a helicopter takes visitors on a flight over the harbour. The viewpoint building on the cliff-tops houses a small exhibition of photographs, and copies of the original plans for constructing the harbour.

Courseulles-sur-Mer

Position 49°20′N 0°27′W.
Charts Admiralty *2073, 1821, 1349* (plan)
    Imray *C32*

General

The fishing port of Courseulles-sur-Mer is famous for its oysters. Since the war it has become a popular seaside resort with blocks of holiday apartments. It is also a busy yachting centre. Demand for berths has grown to such an extent that a new marina has been built in an arm of the river Seulles and Courseulles can now accommodate a total of 800 boats.

The town is quite pleasant in its own way, and has something to satisfy most tastes or needs.

Tidal information

HW at Courseulles is HW Le Havre −0029.

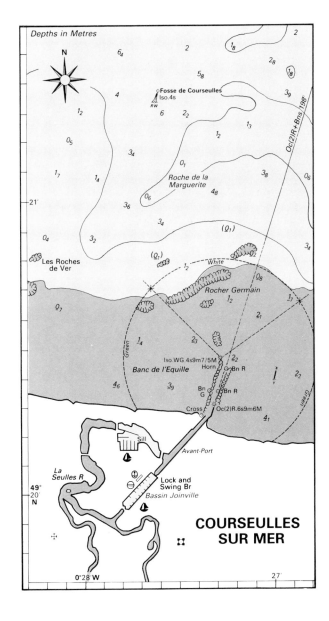

If you arrive too early to lock in it is possible to anchor in the approaches to Courseulles, close southwest of the RW safe-water buoy in depths of about 6m. Beware of a submarine cable just to the west of this anchorage. Closer in there is also an anchorage in a pool 4m deep situated ½ mile southeast of the safe-water buoy. This second anchorage is however very close to a drying rock, and is not as easy to locate. The bottom consists of mud and clay and offers good holding. These anchorages are only tenable in good conditions, or in offshore winds.

Approach

Courseulles is one of the more difficult harbours to identify from seaward. This is not helped by the need to stay about 2 miles offshore to avoid the Plateau du Calvados. 2 miles west of the port is the lighthouse at Pointe de Ver which is partly obscured by trees. In the nearer approach the RW safe-water buoy 1·1 miles north-northwest of the harbour aids positive identification. When approaching this buoy the deepest water will be found by approaching it on a course of 134°. This course is the transit of two church towers. The first church is at Bernières, a coastal village 1·5 miles east of Courseulles. The second church is inland at La Délivrande and has twin towers. Unfortunately this transit is very difficult to spot from the deck of the average yacht because of tall trees.

It is possible to anchor near the safe-water buoy to await sufficient water to enter the harbour. If there is sufficient water to enter the harbour continue on the same bearing from the safe-water buoy until you can see into the harbour entrance. From this point the harbour entrance will be bearing 198°. Head straight for the harbour, allowing for any tidal set across the entrance. Submerged training walls extend in an approximately north-northeast direction from the jetty and the spur. They are marked by a light on a dolphin at the end of the western training wall, and a number of unlit pole beacons. Keep to the east side of the entrance channel when entering. The west side has a tendency to silt up.

Once inside the harbour there is a choice of berth. Either continue straight ahead, through the lock gate and road bridge into the Bassin Joinville or turn to starboard through a swing bridge into the new drying yacht harbour.

Note that it is dangerous to approach or attempt to enter the harbour in strong onshore winds.

Lights
Pointe de Ver Fl(3)15s42m26M RC
Safe-water buoy Iso.4s
W breakwater Iso.WG.4s7m9/5M Horn30s
E breakwater Oc(2)R.6s9m7M

Radiobeacon
Pointe de Ver *ER* 291·9 kHz 20M Seq 5 Cont
　49°20'·5N 0°31'·2W

Height of tide above chart datum
MHWS 7·1m, MHWN 5·6m, MLWN 2·3m, MLWS 0·9m

Tidal streams
In the approach to Courseulles the tidal streams run west on the ebb at up to 1·3 knots, and east-southeast at up to 1·9 knots on the flood. The ebb starts at HW Le Havre +0100 and flows until HW Le Havre −0400, when the flood starts.

Minimum depths
The outer harbour and the approach dry for a distance of ¾ mile offshore. There is just over 2m at LW in the Bassin Joinville (the wet basin), and approximately 1m at LW at the visitors' berth in the new basin.

Timing
The lock gates are open from approximately 2 hours before HW to 2 hours after HW.

The entrance to Courseulles-sur-Mer at low water, viewed from
north.

Leaving Courseulles-sur-Mer at high water.

Port radio
VHF Ch 9.

Berth
Of the two possible berths, either in the Bassin Joinville (through the lock) or in the new basin to starboard, the former offers a better berth. The lock gates open from 2 hours before HW to 2 hours after HW. The bridge across the lock gates opens on demand. Visitors are normally directed to lie alongside the east quay, just beyond the lock. Alternatively it may be possible to tie up bow-to at one of the pontoons.

Access to the berths in the new yacht harbour is possible 3 hours either side of HW. Again the bridge will open on request. The bridge has a central pier and the navigable channel is through the seaward gap. Beware of a strong tidal set flowing under the bridge into the new yacht harbour on a rising tide and the reverse on a falling tide. Visitors should berth at the pontoon which lies alongside the wall to port. Note that in this basin many of the berths only have a metre of water, whilst others dry.

Shelter
There is good all round shelter once inside the Bassin Joinville, although in strong onshore winds a surge is noticeable during the period that the lock gates are open.

Officials
Harbourmaster and customs are located in the *Capitainerie* building on the west side of the Bassin Joinville; harbourmaster ☎ 31 37 51 69. Police in the town. There is a yacht club here.

Harbour dues
Charges are made.

Facilities
Water and electricity are laid onto the pontoons. Fuel is available from a garage in the Rue du Maréchal Foch (just east of the Bassin Joinville) or from a garage on the Route de Ver to the west. Showers are available in the *Capitainerie* building during office hours; you have to obtain a token from the office at a cost of 5fr.

Banks, post office, an excellent selection of shops and supermarkets. There are big markets on Tuesdays and Fridays which fill the main shopping street. Fresh fish is sold from stalls on the quayside. The oyster farm sells live oysters to the public.

Pharmacy, doctors, dentists. There are two well stocked chandleries. Mobile crane. Repairs to hulls, sails and engines are possible. A good choice of restaurants and hotels. Laundrette in the Place du Marché. Tourist information office. Sporting opportunities include swimming (heated seawater pool), riding, bowling and tennis.

Communications
Bus service. Car hire and taxis.

The new marina at Courseulles-sur-Mer lies on the river Seulles. Most of the berths dry.

The best berth at Courseulles-sur-Mer is through the lock in the wet basin, the Bassin Joinville. The visitors' berths are in the foreground, but you may be directed to a vacant berth.

History
This small holiday resort's main historical interest lies in its D-day connection. Courseulles lies at the east end of Juno beach, the Canadian landing zone. During the early part of the landings the beach and harbour were protected by blockships, sunk in the approaches. One example of an amphibious Sherman tank rests on a plinth near the sea front. It is a reminder of the quantities of equipment landed here, before the 'mulberry' harbour at Arromanches was completed.

To see

Juno Beach is now a popular holiday beach, and no visit can be complete without a walk along it. The oyster beds near the harbour are used to mature imported oysters, which are prominent on local restaurant menus. An aquarium and shellfish museum is located on the promenade near the harbour entrance.

Ouistreham

Position 49°17'N 0°15'W
Charts Admiralty *1821, 1349* (plan)
        Imray *C32*

General

The small town of Ouistreham lies at the mouth of the Caen Canal and the Orne river. Once it was just a fishing port, where the tide governed the passage of merchant ships wishing to travel up the river to the city of Caen. Today coasters pass through the sea lock and into the canal which leads to the steel works and factories lying to the north of Caen. Ouistreham still has its fishing fleet, and as from 1986 is the terminal for the new ferry service operated by Brittany Ferries between Ouistreham and Portsmouth.

The fine sandy beach at Ouistreham has led to the town's metamorphosis into a family holiday resort, and its villas, suburban streets and hotels have merged into the adjacent resort of Riva-Bella. The accent is low key. There are several hotels and restaurants, but the boutiques and discos of more sophisticated resorts such as Deauville are missing.

From the yachtsman's point of view there is a well sheltered (and expensive by Norman standards) marina just inside the canal. It is a bit out of the way as far as restaurants and shops are concerned, but this does not seem to affect its popularity.

For us the chief attraction of Ouistreham is that it gives access to the wonderful historic city of Caen.

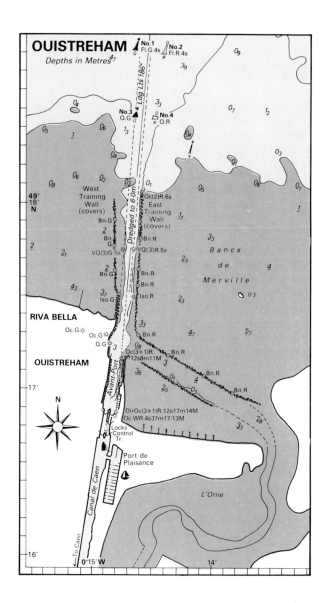

Tidal information

HW at Ouistreham is approximately HW Le Havre −0015, or HW Dover −0115.

Height of tide above chart datum
MHWS 7·7m, MHWN 6·4m, MLWN 2·8m, MLWS 1·0m

Tidal streams
The tidal streams in the approach to Ouistreham run parallel to the coast at up to 1·2 knots on springs. 3 hours before HW Le Havre the tide starts to flow in an east-southeast direction. This continues until 2 hours after HW when it starts to flow in a west-northwest direction.

Minimum depths
There is a minimum depth of 2·6m in the approach channel to Ouistreham. The canal is dredged to 9m.

Timing
The lock gates operate from approximately 2 hours before HW to 3 hours after HW. Note however that the operating times vary depending on tide and season. The exact times of lock operations are posted up at the control tower, and in the marinas at Ouistreham and Caen. If you arrive outside of these times there is a waiting pontoon on the port-hand side of the channel, a short distance from the locks, where you can tie up for up to 7 hours.

Ouistreham. The lock into the ship canal on a busy Sunday afternoon.

The Pont de Bénouville, or Pegasus Bridge, is the first opening bridge on the canal leading up to Caen. A convoy of yachts passes through together.

A surprising number of local yachts are kept on drying moorings at the mouth of the river Orne, near Ouistreham.

Approach

Ouistreham is easily identified in reasonable visibility by the tall lighthouse (a white tower with a red top) which is located on the east side of the lock. On summer weekends the number of yachts sailing in the area will also be a clue.

Approaching from west beware of the rocky coastal plateau which extends for over a mile offshore. There are a number of wrecks in the approach from the northwest, the most dangerous of which are marked by an unlit east cardinal buoy. If approaching from east there is a shallow coastal bank which is extending seaward as the spoil from dredging is dumped. The north edge of this spoil ground is marked by a lit north cardinal buoy. A lit RW safewater buoy marks the start of the fairway. From this buoy a course of 186° leads into the outer harbour. Two leading lights line up on this bearing at night. Beware of a strong tidal crosscurrent which tends to sweep you out of the channel.

It is not necessary for a yacht to enter the channel at the fairway buoy, but beware of shallow depths on either side if you are cutting a corner. Two lit G buoys and two lit R buoys mark the outer part of the channel. The seaward ends of training walls are marked by lit beacons to port and starboard. The walls themselves are marked at intervals by pole beacons surmounted by topmarks. You should certainly be within the channel before you meet the beacons and training walls.

Once within the outer harbour a channel leads off to port into the river Orne and the main channel continues south towards the lock gates. A waiting berth for the use of yachts is situated on the port-hand side, opposite the ferry berth. This waiting pontoon is intended for yachts waiting the next lock opening, but is also useful if waiting for a favourable tide to continue along the coast.

In strong winds and seas from northwest, north and northeast approach and entry can be extremely difficult, if not dangerous.

Beware of ferry traffic in the vicinity of Ouistreham, and note that from the ferry's point of view the channel up to Ouistreham is narrow.

Locking in

There are two large locks at Ouistreham, separated by the port building and lock control tower. Light signals indicate which lock is in use. Entering the lock in the height of summer can be daunting if you have never entered a lock before. The sheer number and speed of other yachts and powerboats, which stampede into the lock as soon as the gates open, is enough to make even the steely nerved blanch. If you find yourself inadvertently in the forefront go as far up the lock as possible, taking care not to hit the low bridge which crosses the eastern lock midway. This is a ship lock, and unfortunately it is not equipped with the modern floating bollards. Rings and bollards at the top of the wall are quite far apart, but there are several ladders. You will probably need to send someone ashore with bow and stern lines.

Once you have tied up you will find other vessels coming alongside you, so have fenders out on both sides, and be prepared to take their lines.

If you are one of the last yachts into the lock, have fenders and lines ready, and tie up alongside another yacht.

Lights

Ouistreham main Lt Oc.WR.4s37m17/13M
Fairway buoy Iso.4s8m4M Whistle
Extremity of E training wall Oc(2)R.6s7m8M
End of W mole Iso.G.4s12m9M Horn10s
Ldg Lts 185° Front DirOc(3+1)R.12s8m9M
  Rear DirOc(3+1)R.12s17m15M

Port radio

VHF Ch 16, 68.

Berth

If you arrive outside of the lock opening times there is a low waiting pontoon on the east side of the channel, north of the fishing-boat berths. At night this should have three individual fixed red lights on it. Yachts are not allowed to tie up for more than 7 hours. This waiting pontoon can also be useful on departure when waiting for a suitable tide to continue on your way. The waiting berth is exposed to winds and seas from seaward and can at times be uncomfortable, if not dangerous.

Once through the lock the marina entrance lies on your port-hand side, just beyond the fuel berth. Note that at night the entrance is not marked by red and green lights as you would expect. The visitors' berth is right opposite the marina entrance. Tie up alongside, as space allows.

On the opposite side of the canal is a quay used by the tugs and fishing boats, and it may be possible to tie up here if space permits.

If you intend going up to Caen there is a quay just before the first opening bridge (Pegasus Bridge or Le Pont de Bénouville) where you can tie up. For the impecunious it has the advantage that you avoid paying marina dues. Make sure that your lines are secure, and that you are well fendered. If a ship passes there can be quite a surge.

River Orne

There are numerous moorings in this river estuary east of the ferry berth. It is possible to anchor here if your yacht can safely take the ground on a bed of shellfish and stones. We have tried it, and do not recommend it. It is quite frightening having a 3 knot current passing under you at the moment you lift off the seabed and swing round to face the flood!

Canal de Caen (Admiralty chart *1349*)

The ship canal leads to the marina at Caen, right in the heart of this delightful city. As you lock into the canal at Ouistreham check the times of the 'convoys' for pleasure vessels, posted at the lock control tower. There is usually a morning and evening convoy each way, the exact time depending on the tides. Whether you wait at Pegasus Bridge (described below) or in the marina you should be at Pegasus Bridge, and obviously awaiting passage, at the appointed time. The convoy, be it one or ten yachts, will be afforded free (no charge) passage through the four bridges to Caen, at the speed of the slowest yacht.

It is also possible to use a horn, to attract the bridge-keeper's attention, and obtain passage when you desire. You will incur a charge for this service, which is payable at the marina office in Caen.

Pegasus Bridge (Pont de Bénouville)

The first bridge across the Caen Canal is 2½ miles from Ouistreham at the village of Bénouville. This is the famous Pegasus Bridge, named after the emblem of the 6th Airborne Division, which mounted the first operation of Overlord, the invasion of Europe in June 1944. The task of the 6th Airborne Division was to capture, intact, the two bridges over the canal and the river Orne.

Just after midnight on the 5th/6th June 1944 (D-day) the troops who were to capture Pegasus Bridge landed in three gliders close to the bridge. Each glider had two pilots, two officers and 28 men on board. The first glider landed with its nose poking through the barbed wire defences surrounding the bridge. The men, led by Major John Howard, piled out and overpowered the German defenders with such speed that the Germans had no opportunity to blow the bridge up. A team of *sapeurs*, who had been included in the party, specifically to defuse the charges, subsequently discovered that the explosives were not in place!

The bridge over the river Orne was captured intact by another task force which also landed in gliders.

The airborne troops successfully defended the bridges until relieved at midday by commandos under the leadership of Lord Lovat. Lord Lovat's arrival was dramatic. He strolled across the bridge, accompanied by his piper, under enemy fire.

Today there is a fascinating museum next to the first house in France to be liberated.

Shelter

Once inside the locks at Ouistreham the marina and canal enjoy good all round shelter.

Officials

The harbour office is located in the lock control tower between the locks, ☎ 31 97 14 43. Information on lock and bridge opening times is posted here. Customs at the ferry terminal. Police in the town. Yacht club at the marina, ☎ 31 97 13 05.

Harbour dues

There are marina charges at Ouistreham. This was the second most expensive marina we visited, the most expensive being Boulogne.

Facilities

Water and electricity laid onto the marina pontoons. Fuel from the fuel berth at the entrance to the marina. Showers in the yacht club (open from 0815 to 1800). Toilets. Several chandleries, and repair facilities for hulls, engines, and sails. Mobile cranes, slips and travel-hoist. Across the canal in Ouistreham basic shopping needs can be met, but choice is limited. Fresh fish, fruit and vegetables are sold on the quayside. Bank, post office, restaurants and hotels. Tourist information in the ferry terminal. Casino, art gallery, cinema, tennis courts, go-carts.

Communications

Ferries to Portsmouth. Bus service. Car hire and taxis.

History

Ouistreham's role as Caen's outlet to the sea has led to some turbulent history. English armies on their way to attack Caen, the former capital of this part of Normandy, often used to disembark at Ouistreham. In 1346 the troops of Edward III of England looted Caen, and their plunder was shipped home to England from Ouistreham. The tables were turned one dark night in July 1762 when a coastguard, Michel Cabien, single-handedly repelled an English attack. He was subsequently rewarded by being promoted to general. His feat is commemorated on a plaque outside the extraordinary wood-framed cinema, named the Salle Cabien.

During the Second World War the Germans built sea defences here, part of their Atlantic Wall. There is a *blockhaus*, still intact, which can be visited near the beach.

To see

Blockhaus and Musée du Débarquement. The church in Ouistreham is Romanesque and Gothic and mainly dates from the twelfth and thirteenth centuries.

It is well worth visiting the museum at Pegasus Bridge (see above).

Approach channel   Ferry (not always there!)   Lighthouse   Ouistreham Church

Ouistreham from 2M northwest.

Caen

Position 49°11'N 0°21'W
Charts Admiralty *1349* (plan)

General

The historic city of Caen has close links with William the Conqueror and hence with the history of England. It is renowned for its green and pleasant aspect, although it is also an important industrial centre and one of France's more important ports.

Although most of Caen was destroyed by Allied bombardment during the Second World War the city was restored sympathetically, and many of its historic buildings can be visited today. The yachtsman can enjoy the advantages of being right in the centre of the city. Despite its location the marina is surprisingly quiet and secure.

It is certainly worthwhile making the detour up the Canal de Caen and spending a few days soaking up the atmosphere and culture on offer.

Berth

A visiting yacht has little choice but to use the berths provided at the marina, but you can hardly complain. After all they are right in the heart of the city!

Officials

Convoy times and Ouistreham lock operating hours, as well as weather information, are obtainable from the marina office, ☎ 31 93 74 47. The customs office is on the Quai Vendeuvre (opposite the marina).

Harbour dues

Dues are payable for every 24-hour period, or part thereof. This therefore means that if you arrive at say 4pm one day and want to leave with the following afternoon convoy you will be liable for two days dues, because the convoy will leave approximately one hour later on the next day.

Facilities

Water and electricity at the marina. There is only one shower, but you do not have to pay extra for its use. Toilets. Banks, post office, an excellent selection of shops plus all the facilities of a major city are close at hand. Large Sunday market on the quayside opposite the marina. Fuel from a petrol station adjacent to the marina. Two laundrettes, one near the petrol station and one near the church of St-Jean. Doctors, dentists, pharmacies and a hospital.

Communications

Railway station and bus service. Car hire and taxis. Ferries to Portsmouth from Ouistreham. Airport.

History

Caen owes its historic importance to William the Conqueror, who recognised its strategic importance. He also chose Caen as the site of the Abbaye aux Hommes, which he built as a penance for marrying his cousin, Matilda. The Pope so disapproved of the marriage, because of the close blood relationship, that he excommunicated the newlyweds. Excommunication was not only a religious problem for William, but also politically undesirable since it gave carte blanche to any rivals to attempt to depose him.

The excommunication was withdrawn after William's friend, the priest and future Archbishop of Canterbury, Lanfranc, had negotiated with the Pope on their behalf. As penance William and Matilda founded four hospitals (at Caen, Rouen, Cherbourg and Bayeux) and the Abbaye aux Hommes and the Abbaye aux Dames in Caen. Fortunately both abbeys survived the Second World War and are major landmarks in modern Caen.

The mellow limestone for which Caen is famous was used by William for the construction of Canterbury Cathedral and the Tower of London. The stone was so desirable that Henry V prohibited its use in Normandy and England for secular buildings, which explains the prominence of timber framed

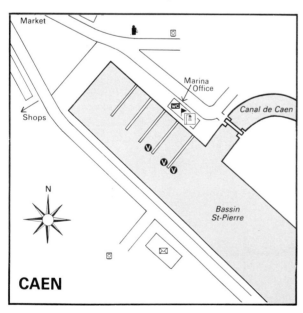

The skyline of Caen, a town which arose phoenix-like out of the ashes of the Second World War. Many of the historic buildings have been restored, and the town has been rebuilt sympathetically.

buildings in medieval Caen. During the Second World War a large number of the people of Caen took shelter in the underground quarries to the south of the city from which Caen stone had been quarried for centuries.

Although William the Conqueror died in Rouen he was buried in his Abbaye aux Hommes. The tomb had such symbolic significance that it was twice despoiled, first by the Huguenots in the sixteenth century and then by the revolutionaries in 1793. William's remains have been lost forever.

During the Hundred Years War Edward III of England besieged Caen. The city was taken in 1346, and because of the burghers' refusal to pay him feudal dues, Edward sacked the city. One hundred ships sailed from Ouistreham heavily laden with the booty.

1417 again saw Englishmen attacking Caen. The city was captured in 1417 by Henry V and remained in English hands until 1450. English occupation was however not all bad. The new governor and regent of Normandy, the Duke of Bedford, founded Caen University in 1432.

During the nineteenth century there was a considerable English community living in Caen. In 1830 the English dandy and former leader of fashion, Beau Brummell (1778–1840), was made British Consul at Caen. His consulship only lasted two years before he was imprisoned (briefly) because of his debts. His last years were marred by insanity, but he was cared for by the nuns of Bon-Sauveur.

Although much of Caen was destroyed by Allied bombing during the invasion of Normandy in 1944, the two abbeys were deliberately spared. The French resistance managed to let the Allies know that civilians had taken refuge there, and that the buildings were being used as hospitals.

To see

There is so much to see in Caen that it is worth buying a guide to the city or asking for advice and a town map at the tourist information office.

The Abbaye aux Hommes is now the city hall. Guided tours are provided. It is also possible to visit the abbey church of St-Etienne which is considered to be one of Caen's wonders. The Abbaye aux Dames houses local government offices, but there are again guided tours.

Another major church, St-Pierre (near the marina), was hit by a shell from *HMS Rodney*. This demolished the belfry, but it has since been reconstructed. Despite the heavy bombing a few old buildings still survive.

A good example of a medieval timber-framed town house which survived now contains the Musée de la Poste et des Techniques de Communication.

The castle, is surrounded by twelfth, thirteenth, and fourteenth-century walls and contains the remains of William's keep. These walls enclose a park as well as two museums. The Musée des Beaux Arts contains an exceptional collection of paintings, whilst the Musée Ethnographique houses a collection depicting the history of rural Normandy. There is also the Jardin des Simples which has a collection of medieval medicinal and aromatic herbs.

The marina at Caen is located in the Bassin St Pierre, right in the centre of the city.

Cabourg and Dives-sur-Mer

Position 49°18′N 0°05′W

Charts Admiralty *2613, 2146, 1821*
Imray *C32, C31*

General

The small towns of Cabourg and Dives are situated on either side of the tidal river Dives. Cabourg is very much a holiday resort with a long sandy beach. Despite its associations with Marcel Proust, who was a frequent visitor at the turn of the century, there are many modern holiday apartment blocks as well as buildings in a more traditional style. Dives on the other hand has a small fishing fleet, a large and conspicuous factory, and is altogether less frivolous.

Tidal information

HW at Dives is HW Le Havre −0055.

Height of tide above chart datum
MHWS 7·5m, MHWN 6·1m, MLWN 2·4m, MLWS 0·9m

Tidal streams
The tidal streams run parallel to the coast. Off the entrance to Dives the current runs at up to 1·2 knots on springs. Within the river the current runs strongly, particularly on the flood when it can reach 5 knots on springs. The ebb reaches about 2¾ knots on springs.

Minimum depths
All the berths at Cabourg and Dives dry.

Timing
The river can be entered two hours either side of HW by a yacht drawing 1m. The best time to enter or leave, however, is near HW when the tide is slack.

Approach

The river entrance lies to the west of the distinctive reddish cliffs, the Falaises des Vaches Noires. To the west of the estuary the countryside is flat and generally low lying, whilst wooded slopes lie close east and southeast. The adjoining villages of Houlgate, Dives and Cabourg show up well at the point where the hills come down to the river plain.

The entrance to the river Dives from seaward. The port-hand and starboard-hand buoys can just be made out.

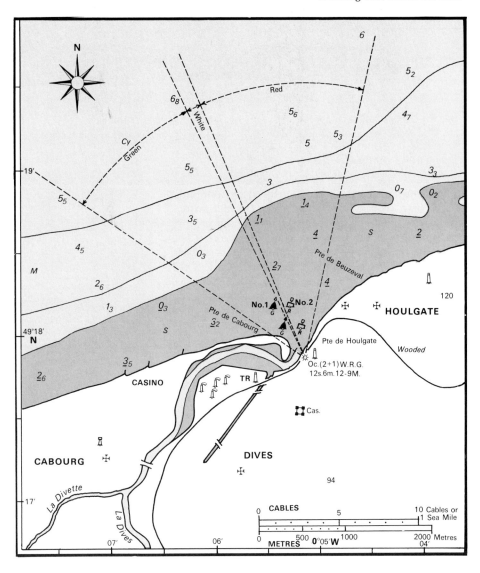

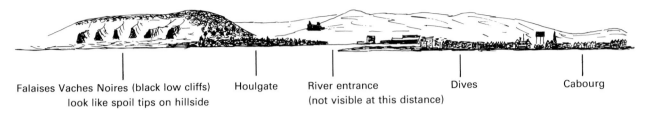

Falaises Vaches Noires (black low cliffs) | Houlgate | River entrance | Dives | Cabourg
look like spoil tips on hillside | | (not visible at this distance) | |

Cabourg, Dives and Houlgate from NW, 2M off.

The entrance to the river is marked by four unlit buoys, two red and two green. The channel swings round to the west and passes close to the railway embankment at the base of the wooded slopes. The edges of the channel are marked by perches. Note that shallow water extends east from the end of the sandy spit on the west side of the entrance. Once round this spit the river widens to form a wide and flat area where moorings have been laid. The quay at Dives lies immediately ahead, whilst the river channel curves round to hug the north shore. The moorings and pontoons of Cabourg are about 1 mile up the river.

Although there is a sectored light marking the entrance, entry at night is not advisable. Approach and entry should not be attempted in strong onshore winds.

Lights

Dives-sur-Mer   Oc(2+1)WRG.12s6m12-9M   124°-G-154°-W-157°-R-193°

Berth

The best bet at Dives is to enquire whether it would be possible to tie up at the sailing club pontoon. The quay is used by the fishing boats, and lying alongside here could be difficult. It is also possible to anchor close under the sand dunes of Cap Cabourg, north of the quay at Dives.

If you continue up to the yacht club at Cabourg it is possible to lie alongside one of their pontoons, but again seek permission.

Shelter

Once inside the shelter is good.

Officials

Police in the towns. Yacht clubs in both Dives and Cabourg: Société Houlgataise des Régates de la Dives (for mooring at Dives) ☎ 31 91 47 10; Cabourg Yacht Club ☎ 31 91 28 89.

Facilities

At Dives there is a water tap and hose at the top of the pontoon and another tap on the side of the building near the fish quay. The nearest source of petrol is about 10 minutes walk from the quay, at a filling station on the road to Cabourg. There is a supermarket here as well, but other shops are even further away. Fresh fish is sold on the quay. There

Dives. The yacht club's pontoon lies beyond the fishing-boat quay.

is a bar and telephone box nearby. Bank, post office, tourist information office and shops are in the town.

At Cabourg water and electricity are laid onto the club pontoons, but there is no fuel nearby. The yacht club has a new building with toilets and showers. On the ground floor of the nearby apartment block are a number of shops, including a bakery. Other shops can be found in the town which also has a casino, tourist information office, golf course, hotels and restaurants. Immediately next door to the yacht club is Cabourg Marine. The yard can undertake various repairs, is an agent for Yanmar and Nannidiesel, and has a mobile crane.

Communications

Bus service. Railway station at Dives. Car hire and taxis.

History

In 1001 a wooden statue of Christ was washed ashore near Dives-sur-Mer. This statue, called the Sanctus Salvator, is said by some sources to be the origin for the name, Calvados, the name of the region. Other sources, however, claim that a Spanish vessel, the *San Salvador*, which was wrecked on the rocks lying off this coast is the true origin of the name Calvados. Be that as it may the old name for Dives was St-Sauver.

Yacht club moorings and pontoons at Cabourg, on the river Dives.

River moorings at Cabourg.

Before the river silted up Dives was one of the most important ports in this area. Dives' main claim to fame is that it was at this port that William the Conqueror's fleet assembled for its invasion of England in 1066; the harbour must have been quite large because the fleet had to carry 250,000 troops! The great fleet left Dives in the summer, only to be dispersed by a fierce storm. Many of the ships were wrecked. Some of the surviving fleet limped into St-Valéry-sur-Somme to seek shelter, and it was from there that they finally departed for England.

Cabourg was developed as a holiday resort in the middle of the nineteenth century when sea bathing gained popularity. The construction of the railway added impetus to this development, as Cabourg was brought within easy reach of Parisians. The asthmatic writer Marcel Proust spent many summer holidays here and at other resorts in Normandy. His memories and experiences of these holidays, the people he met, and the places fused together to create the resort of Balbec. Whether he would recognise the Cabourg of today is another matter.

To see

In the late Gothic church of Notre-Dame-de-Dives is a list of the nobles who are supposed to have accompanied William the Conqueror on his invasion of England. This list was only erected in 1862. The church used to be a place of pilgrimage. There is an interesting medieval market hall, at least four hundred years old, in Dives.

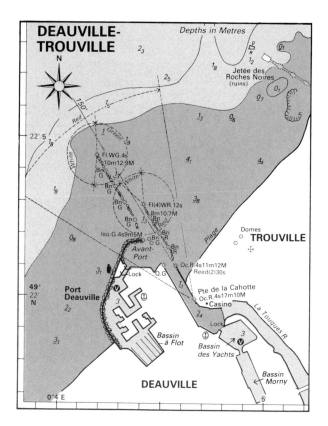

Trouville and Deauville

Position 49°22′N 0°05′E
Charts Admiralty *2613, 2146, 1349* (plan)
　　　　Imray *C32, C31*

General

The neighbouring towns of Trouville and Deauville lie on either side of the river Touques. Both are holiday resorts with fine sandy beaches, bright beach umbrellas, wooden changing huts, and the famous *planches*, teak boardwalks laid over the sand at the top of the beaches. Deauville is considered the more fashionable resort and has prices to match. Trouville on the other hand seems more like a town that is lived in.

The yachtsman can choose to berth either at the marina at Deauville, or in the yacht basin at Trouville, actually located on the Deauville side of the river. In practice you may find you have no choice but to go to the marina, since the lock gates into Trouville basin open for a comparatively short time. The prices at Deauville marina are quite reasonable, in fact they are only slightly higher than the cost of berthing in Trouville.

Besides being a popular yacht harbour, there is quite a large fishing fleet based here. The majority of the fleet berths alongside quays lining the river.

Tidal information

HW Le Havre −0033 (springs), or −0013 (neaps). Dover −0130.

Height of tide above chart datum
MHWS 7·8m, MHWN 6·4m, MLWN 2·8m, MLWS 1·1m

Tidal streams
Tidal streams run parallel to the coast at rates of up to 3 knots on springs. The E-going flood starts at HW Le Havre −0540. The W-going ebb starts at HW Le Havre −0055. Tides flowing into the harbour reach 2¾ knots whilst the ebb tide reaches 1¾ knots. Beware of turbulence at the entrance to Trouville yacht basin. The entrance to the lock into Deauville marina is in a tidal backwater.

Minimum depths
The entrance to the harbour dries 2·4m above chart datum. Access is difficult in onshore winds when waves break within the channel. There is a minimum depth of 3m in the yacht harbour at Trouville and 2·4m in Deauville marina.

The entrance to the harbours of Deauville and Trouville.

The lock into the marina at Deauville is busy, particularly at weekends when yachts are packed in like the proverbial sardines. In this photograph there is plenty of room to spare!

Deauville marina.

Approach

In strong onshore winds it is dangerous to approach or attempt to enter this port.

Approaching from the west there are no dangers except the generally shallow nature of this part of the coast. From the direction of Le Havre or the north take care to avoid the various banks surrounding the entrance to the river Seine. There are a number of lit cardinal buoys which assist navigation. In the nearer approach the west cardinal buoy named *Trouville SW* will be found 1 mile west-northwest of the harbour entrance. Should there be insufficient water for you to enter it is possible, assuming good conditions, to anchor somewhere within the vicinity of this buoy or further east in depths of 2 to 3m (sand and mud) at LW.

An unlit red buoy, 6 cables northeast of the eastern breakwater head marks the seaward end of a ruined jetty which is submerged at HW.

The harbour entrance can be identified by the large cream-coloured building of Trouville casino immediately to the east, and the breakwater, apartment blocks and yacht masts at Deauville marina to the west.

The entrance channel lies between submerged training walls. The outer end of each wall is marked by a lit platform. The walls themselves are marked at intervals by unlit pole beacons. Leading lights in line on 150° assist entry at night. Beware of a strong crosscurrent.

Once within the shelter of the marina breakwater there is a choice between turning to starboard to enter the marina, or continuing straight on between the original harbour breakwaters to the Bassin des Yachts (Trouville harbour).

A small passenger ferry plies across the river near the entrance to the the Bassin des Yachts.

Timing

The lock into Deauville marina is operated from approximately 3 hours before HW to 3 hours after HW. The Trouville lock gate is open from 1½ hours before HW to 2 hours after HW.

Lights

Trouville SW west cardinal buoy VQ(9)10s
End of W training wall Fl.WG.4s10m12/9M
End of E training wall Fl(4)WR.12s8m10/7M
Marina breakwater Iso.G.4s9m5M
W breakwater Q.G.11m9M
Ldg Lts 150° Front (E breakwater) Oc.R.4s11m12M
  Reed(2)30s
Rear (Pte de la Cahotte) Oc.R.4s17m10M

Port radio

VHF Ch 9.

Berth

To berth at Deauville marina turn to starboard inside the entrance. Entrance to the marina is through the lock which operates 3 hours either side of HW. Within the lock there are floating bollards for the use of yachts. Be prepared with plenty of fenders on both sides, and lines. The lock is extremely busy at weekends, and yachts pack into it like the proverbial sardines. If you have to use this lock at the weekend you can avoid the crush (literally) by waiting until the tide rises. Both sets of gates are opened at around 1½ hours before HW allowing a free flow of vessels in and out. Take care since you may not be able to see the yacht coming the other way as you enter the lock.

Once through the lock the visitors' berths are on the pontoon to starboard. Tie up alongside this. A marina official will call on you to collect your dues. Take no notice of the sign at the lock; there is no need to go up to the lock-keeper for permission to enter.

If you wish to go to the Trouville Bassin des Yachts the single lock gate opens from 1½ hours before HW to 2 hours after HW. The visitors' berths are alongside the floating pontoon in the far southeast corner of the first basin, the Bassin des Yachts.

Fishing boats tie up alongside the quays in the river. None of these berths are suitable for yachts, and are not recommended. In parts there are stone ledges which could cause a yacht to lean over as the tide drops, and there is also a lot of rubbish, including supermarket trolleys. If you arrive too late to enter the marina, it is possible to dry out near the marina lock gate, but only if you can take the ground safely.

Shelter

Although the entrance is dangerous in strong onshore winds the harbour offers excellent shelter in either basin. The only disadvantage being that if the weather is really rough the visitors' berths at Deauville marina will be pretty miserable.

At Trouville the visitors' berths are on the far side of this basin, where the sign is.

Officials

The customs officials at Deauville and Trouville are particularly zealous and you can be sure to receive a visit. Their office is at 2 Rue Decaens, near the Pont des Belges, on the Deauville side of the river. Representatives of the harbour office or marina will also call to collect their dues. Weather forecasts are posted up at the harbour/marina offices. Deauville marina ☎ 31 98 30 01 and Trouville harbourmaster ☎ 31 88 28 71. The locations of their various offices are shown on the plan. Police in the town.

Harbour dues

Charges are similar at Deauville marina and the Bassin des Yachts in Trouville.

Facilities

Deauville marina Water and electricity are laid onto the visitors' pontoon. Petrol and diesel from the fuel berth on the starboard-hand side, between the lock and the visitors' pontoon. Showers and toilets are located some distance away on the far south side of the marina.

Trouville Water on the visitors' pontoon. Showers and toilets on the quayside nearby. Petrol is available from a fuel berth on the far side of the inner basin. Diesel is available at the garage serving the fuel berth but has to be collected in containers.

Both Deauville and Trouville have an excellent range of shops, and supermarkets, hotels and restaurants. Those in Trouville are on average cheaper, especially in the back streets. Sunday markets in Deauville and Trouville (the latter has the better vegetable and fruit market). Banks, post offices, tourist information offices. Laundrette at the junction of Rue Victor Hugo and Rue de la Chapelle in Trouville (quite a hike).

Swimming pools, tennis courts, riding, golf, mini golf, go-carts, cinemas, casinos, race course (Deauville), art galleries. Hospital, pharmacies, doctors and dentists.

Chandleries. Travel-lift at Deauville marina. Several yards specialise in repairing yacht hulls. Engine and sail repairs.

Communications

Railway station and bus service. Car hire and taxis. Airport with regular flights to London (Gatwick) during the summer season. Bicycle hire (Pouchin, 11 Quai de la Marine).

History

The fishing village of Trouville became a fashionable resort during the mid-nineteenth century and was visited by most of the prominent painters of the era, as well as by a number of famous literary figures such as Dumas and Flaubert. There is a statue of Flaubert on the quayside at Trouville.

The fishing fleet at Trouville moors alongside the quays lining the river Touques (looking downstream). Yachts should moor within the wet basin at Trouville or in the marina at Deauville.

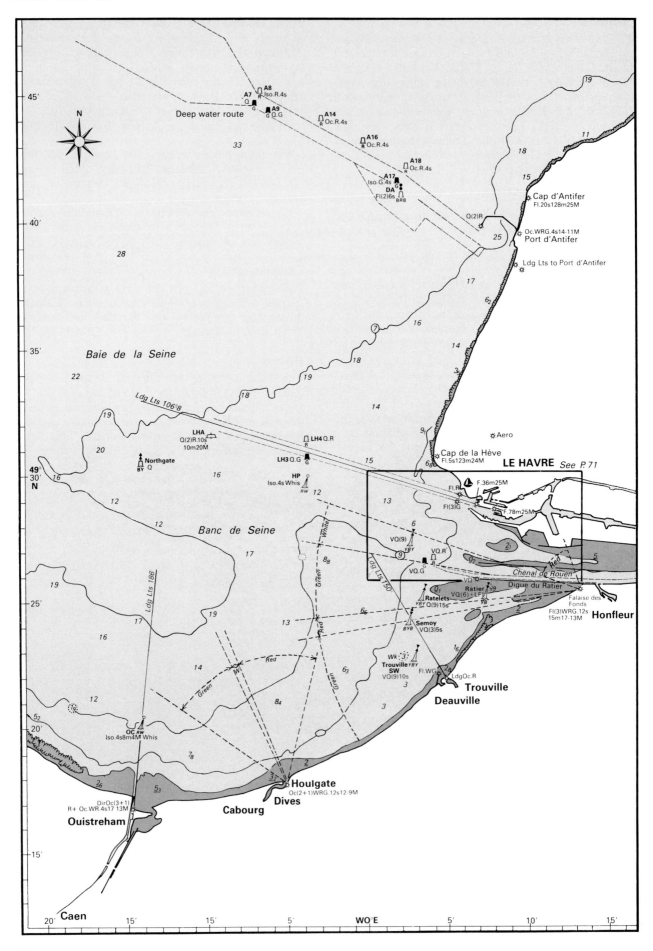

The famous *planches* (boardwalk) at Deauville.

Deauville was a creation of the Duke de Morny, half brother of the Emperor Napoléon III. He was a very successful speculator and succeeded in promoting Deauville as the place for fashionable Parisians to be seen. Deauville retains its air of fashionable elegance to this day.

The nineteenth century was not only a time of pleasure seeking but also a time of political turmoil. When the king, Louis Philippe, was deposed in 1848 he took refuge in a house in Trouville, before making his escape to England via Honfleur. Later, in 1870, the Empress Eugénie, wife of Napoléon III (who had been captured and deposed by the Prussians), fled from Trouville on board a British yacht.

To see

Aquarium and museum at Trouville; the famous Promenades des Planches at Deauville. Swimming pool. The tourist information offices will happily provide you with information on cultural events and other entertainment.

Honfleur

Position 49°25′N 0°14′E
Charts Admiralty *2613, 2146, 2994*
    Imray *C32, C31*

General

The charm of the historic town of Honfleur, clustered around its harbour, has been appreciated by generations of painters. Today Honfleur attracts tourists of all nationalities, and rightly so. If you are cruising in this area the detour into the Seine estuary is well rewarded by the excellent berth in the very heart of the old town. After seeing the sights there can be no better place to relax than on your own boat, only yards from the Lieutenance and the quaint slate hung houses bedecked with bright geraniums. As you sip your wine and savour the atmosphere you can watch the rest of the world go by.

Tidal information

Much of the Seine estuary experiences double high waters on spring tides, and a long stand on HW neaps. On spring tides the first HW at Honfleur occurs 1½ hours before HW Le Havre, and the second HW 1½ hours after HW Le Havre. On neap tides HW at Honfleur can be up to 40 minutes after HW Le Havre.

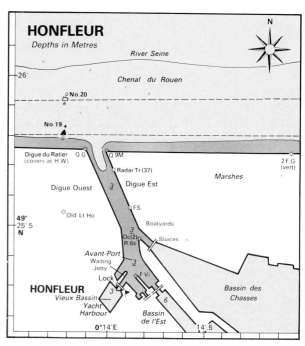

Crowds gather to watch yachts entering and leaving the Vieux Bassin at Honfleur whenever the road bridge opens.

Height of tide above chart datum

MHWS 8·1m, MHWN 6·7m, MLWN 3·0m, MLWS 1·2m

Tidal streams

The tidal streams in the Seine in the approach to Honfleur are strong and must be taken into account. On springs the tide in the Seine can reach up to 4½ knots. Beware of the tide carrying you past the entrance to Honfleur. Caution is also called for when re-entering the river from Honfleur.

The ebb starts to flow out of the Seine at HW Le Havre +0100.

On spring tides (over 7·4m) the approach channel to Honfleur is sluiced for 5 hours around the bottom of the tide.

Minimum depths

The approach channel dries on spring tides, although it is usually possible to dry out in the outer harbour, to await the next locking. The locked Vieux Bassin maintains a depth of 2·8m.

Timing

The lock gates into the inner basin at Honfleur are open from 1 hour before HW (Honfleur) to 1 hour after HW in winter, or 2 hours after HW in summer. The road bridge across the lock opens on HW, and approximately 1 hour before HW, and 1 and 2 hours after HW during daylight hours. At night the bridge only opens once after HW. The exact times of the bridge openings are posted up at the Lieutenance, the old building immediately to the west of the lock and bridge.

You should arrive in good time so that the bridge keeper realises that you want to enter. If you have to wait, tie up temporarily alongside the quay near the bridge.

Approach

When approaching the Seine estuary from seaward beware of the banks to the north and south of the shipping channel to Rouen. These banks have built up around the training walls which constrain the tidal streams to the channel. The seaward ends of these banks are well buoyed, but since there are so many buoys in this area close attention to the chart is required. Any approach to Honfleur, whether from Deauville-Trouville, Le Havre or from seaward, must be made by entering the Chenal de Rouen in the vicinity of buoys No. 5 and No. 6. East of these buoys there are extensive shoal areas and submerged training walls on either side of the channel. These training walls could be dangerous to yachts, even at HW.

Once in the Chenal de Rouen the ship channel is marked by buoys, and the training walls by pole beacons. It is possible to use most of the channel between the training walls, but keep an eye on your echo sounder, and avoid the shallower areas, which lie close to the north training wall.

Take care to keep out of the way of shipping, which has right of way in this confined channel, and which tends to be fast moving.

Approximately 5 miles from the outer end of the trained channel you will find a small canal leading south to Honfleur. The entrance to this canal is easy to identify because of the tall white control tower which lies on the east side of the entrance. The control tower, which regulates the movement of shipping up and down the Chenal de Rouen, has two large radar scanners and is unmistakable.

The tidal stream in the approach canal to Honfleur is much reduced. On departure from Honfleur beware of ships in the main channel. They tend to keep close to this southern shore, and can be hidden from sight by the banks.

The Vieux Bassin, where visitors berth, lies at the end of this canal on the starboard side, about a third of a mile from the entrance. Access is through a lock and bridge.

Lights

Falaise des Fonds Fl(3)WRG.12s15m17-13M
W side of canal entrance Q.G.10m6M
E side of canal entrance Q.9m9M Reed(5)40s
Jetée Est Oc(2)R.6s7m12M

Port radio

VHF Ch 11, 73.

Berth

Visitors berth in the Vieux Bassin. On entering the basin you will be directed to a berth alongside a low pontoon lying on your starboard side. In the season visitors can lie six abreast here! Because of the harbour's popularity visiting yachts may not stay for more than 7 nights.

Shelter

The Vieux Bassin is surrounded by tall buildings and offers extremely good shelter. The Avant-Port is subject to surge in strong northwesterlies.

Officials

The harbourmaster's office is located in the Lieutenance, ☎ 31 89 20 02. Bridge and lock opening times as well as weather forecasts are posted here. Customs office is situated on the Quai Lepaulmier at the junction with Rue Villey. Police in the town. The yacht club supervises and collects visitors' dues. They also provide visitors with a useful booklet listing all the facilities available in the town, and containing a tide table.

Facilities

Water and electricity are laid onto the visitors' pontoon. Fuel is available to yachts at HW only from the fuel berth on the Quai du Transit near the entrance to the Bassin de l'Est. If this is inconvenient there are filling stations on the outskirts of town. There is a good selection of shops, including supermarkets, close at hand. Fruit and vegetable market on Saturday mornings. A colourful flower market is held on Saturdays in the Place Arthur-Boudin. Fresh fish sold daily on the quay. On the Rue de la République there is a particularly good bakery selling many varieties of brown bread. Banks, post office, tourist information office. Showers are available at the swimming pool. Laundrette at 17 Rue Cachin, off the Rue de la République.

There are any number of restaurants, art galleries and craft shops to tempt you to open your wallet, all close to the boat.

Doctors and dentists. The nearest hospital is at Equemauville.

Repairs to engine and hull are possible. No sailmaker or chandlers.

The quaint old houses clustered around the harbour and mirrored in its waters make Honfleur a painter's paradise.

Communications

Bus service. Car hire and taxis. Bicycle hire from Mario Grégory, 12 Quai Lepaulmier.

History

Prior to the fourteenth century little definite is known about the history of Honfleur. It was probably a fishing port, and the name seems to indicate that it was once settled by Scandinavians or Saxons. After the Norman Conquest Honfleur became one of the main ports through which merchandise for England passed.

Honfleur, built at the mouth of the Seine, occupied a strategically important position. Together with Harfleur on the other side of the estuary it controlled trade up and down the Seine, and safeguarded Paris from seaborne enemies.

During the Hundred Years War in the fourteenth century Honfleur's strategic importance was recognised by both sides. The town was fortified by the French king, Charles V, and it also served as a base from which attacks against the English were launched. The English managed to capture the town in 1419 and held onto it until 1450. During the Hundred Years War large parts of the town were damaged, and nothing remains from prior to this period. The small church of St-Etienne, overlooking the Vieux Bassin, was completed during the English occupation on the orders of Henry VI, and is the oldest building in Honfleur.

After the Hundred Years War ended there was a period of relative stability during which the town was rebuilt. Initially the emphasis was on repairing the fortifications, and the war-damaged church of St-Catherine which had been built of stone was replaced by a wooden structure. It has been suggested that the people of Honfleur could not afford stone after all they had suffered during the wars. The wood for the church came from a nearby forest and the work was carried out by local shipwrights and carpenters during the second half of the fifteenth century.

The sixteenth century was a period of growing prosperity, thanks to discoveries in the New World. A number of Honfleur seamen discovered new lands. For example in 1503 Binot Paulmier de Gonneville discovered Brazil, whilst three years later another native of Honfleur travelled to Newfoundland and explored the mouth of the Saint Lawrence. This was the beginning of a long connection with Canada, culminating in the voyage of Samuel Champlain from Honfleur in 1608 which led to the founding of Quebec.

Honfleur ships travelled far and wide to trade or fish. Salt was essential for the fishermen who travelled as far as the Grand Banks in search of cod. An old salt warehouse was replaced in 1670 by three large warehouses on the orders of Colbert. Two of these warehouses still exist, and have been restored.

During the nineteenth century Honfleur began a new phase in its history when it attracted the new Impressionist painters. Eugin Boudin, a local painter whose father had been the master of the Honfleur to Le Havre packet boat, invited his friends and fellow artists to stay at the Ferme St-Simeon just outside the town. It is now an exclusive restaurant revelling in its illustrious past. The municipal art museum is named after Eugin Boudin.

To see

You cannot avoid the most impressive sights in Honfleur, the rows of seven-storey houses surrounding the Vieux Bassin, since you will be moored among them! Do not miss visiting the wooden church of St-Catherine and its separate bell tower. Even if you normally avoid churches, you will be impressed.

The church of St-Etienne, on the quayside, is now a maritime museum. It provides an insight into the developments around this old harbour since the Middle Ages. Nearby, based in the former prison and some sixteenth-century houses, there is a folk museum which has rooms depicting life in past centuries. Unfortunately admission is restricted to conducted tours in French. The Eugin Boudin museum and art gallery has some interesting exhibits and paintings; it is worth a visit if time permits.

You may also enjoy visiting the many art galleries around the old town – one even specialises in ship models.

There are many other sights to see, not least the streets of old half-timbered houses. The local tourist information office produces informative maps and leaflets, and can also give you details of guided tours around Honfleur.

Le Havre

Position 49°29′N 0°06′E
Charts Admiralty *2990* (plan), *2613, 2146*
   Imray *C31, C32*

General

Le Havre is a major city and important deep-water commercial port situated at the mouth of the Seine. There is a large marina within the port close to the entrance. Since access is possible at any state of tide and in all weather conditions, you will inevitably be drawn into using this harbour at some stage of your cruise along this coast.

On first acquaintance Le Havre seems soulless, but with time and plenty of sunshine it could grow on you. Most things that the yachtsman could want or need are available somewhere within the city.

Tidal information

Standard port. HW Le Havre is HW Dover −0100. Note that there is a three hour tidal stand at HW.

Height of tide above chart datum
MHWS 7·9m, MHWN 6·6m, MLWN 3·0m, MLWS 1·2m

Tidal streams
There are strong tidal streams in the approach to Le Havre. Direction and strength are governed by tides flowing into and out of the Seine Estuary. The streams 1 mile off the harbour entrance are:
HW Le Havre the stream flows north at 1 knot on springs.
HW Le Havre +0300 the stream flows northwest at 1·8 knots on springs.
HW Le Havre +0600 the stream is slack.
HW Le Havre −0300 the stream flows southeast at 1·7 knots on springs.

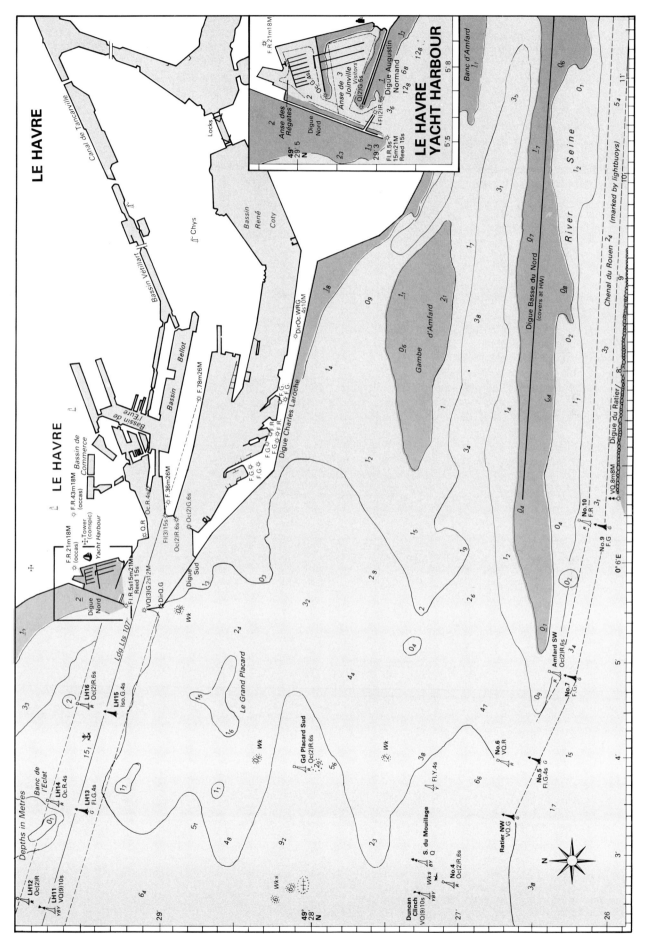

LE HAVRE

LE HAVRE YACHT HARBOUR

Minimum depths

There is a minimum depth of 15m in the buoyed approach channel, whilst the commercial docks are dredged to 12m. Depths in the yacht harbour are maintained at 3m.

Approach

The harbour can be approached in all weather conditions and at any state of tide. Note however that strong winds against the tide create heavy seas in the approach, and that there are tidal eddies at the actual entrance to the harbour.

The approach from seaward is straightforward. There are no natural dangers, but there is a measuring platform, *Parfond*, surrounded by cardinal buoys situated 15 miles west of the port. The buoyed channel starts at the *LHA* lanby some 11 miles offshore. There is no need for a yacht to follow the buoyed channel from seaward. On the other hand the numerous buoys form an excellent landfall for a yacht. Once you have found the channel you need only follow its edge into the harbour. In the final approach beware of a shallow bank, Banc de l'Eclat, just north of the main channel.

From north beware of deep-draught vessels using the buoyed channel to the deep-water berths at Port d'Antifer. There are also two wrecks and a spoil ground which have shallow depths over them. Two of these dangers are marked by light buoys, but the third, halfway between Cap d'Antifer and Le Havre, and 1 mile offshore, is unmarked. Approaching from the Seine or Deauville beware of the shoals which extend between the harbour entrance and the submerged training walls of the Chenal de Rouen.

Note that ships have right of way in all of these buoyed channels. Le Havre is a busy ferry and commercial port, and the River Seine is a major waterway with large ships en route between the sea and Rouen. The port signals, displayed prominently, must be obeyed.

The city and port are conspicuous with their large fuel storage tanks, tall buildings, and two tall chimneys with red and white bands painted on their tops – you really cannot miss Le Havre! The harbour entrance can be located by the huge brown church tower nearby and the white signal tower at the entrance itself.

Once inside the main harbour entrance turn immediately to port past the new pipework breakwater which protects the marina. The visitors' berths are in the first basin, the Anse de Joinville, on the first, outer pontoon. A speed limit of 3 knots applies within the marina area.

The Anse de Joinville at Le Havre. The visitors' berths are on both sides of the first pontoon (in the foreground). The spire of St Joseph's in the background is an excellent landmark.

The yacht clubs at Le Havre have clubhouses overlooking the inner basin, the Anse des Régates.

Lights

Cap d'Antifer Fl.20s128m29M RC
LHA lanby Q(2)R.10s10m20M RC
Cap de la Hève Fl.5s123m24M
N breakwater Fl.R.5s15m21M Horn 15s
S Breakwater VQ(3)G.2s15m11M
Ldg Lts 106·8° DirF.36m25M and DirF.78m25M
Marina E breakwater Q(2)G.5s5m2M
Marina wavebreak Fl(2)R.6s

The slipway at the head of the yacht harbour, the Anse des Régates, at Le Havre.

Radiobeacons

Cap d'Antifer *TI* 291·9 kHz 50M Seq 3 Cont
  49°41'·1N 0°10'E
Le Havre, Octeville Aero RC *LHO* 346 kHz 15M
  Cont 49°35'·8N 0°11'E
LHA lanby *LH* 291·9 kHz 30M Seq 4 Cont
  49°31'·7N 0°09'·8W

Port radio

VHF Ch 9.

Berth

The visitors' berths are on either side of the first outer pontoon in the Anse de Joinville. Tie up bow-to where space permits. There are low finger pontoons for taking stern lines. The marina has berths for yachts of up to 16m in length.

Shelter

There is some surge in the marina, but this is mainly caused by the fishing boats. The new wavebreak at the marina entrance is designed to reduce the amount of swell entering the marina in strong onshore winds.

Officials

Harbourmaster at Boulevard Clemenceau, customs at 201 Boulevard de Strasbourg, police and yacht clubs. A marina official comes to the boat to collect harbour dues, marina ☎ 35 22 72 72. There is a British Consul at 9 Quai George V, ☎ 35 42 27 47.

Facilities

Water and electricity are laid onto the visitors' pontoon. Fuel (petrol and diesel) is available from the fuel berth in the corner of the outer part of the marina area (Anse de Joinville). At LW the ladder up to the fuel pumps is slippery. Showers and toilets in the yacht clubs.

All basic provisions can be obtained within two blocks of the marina. A handy map at the head of the quay shows where the nearest shops are to be found. There is a better range of shops as well as the market a little further in, but still within 20 minutes walk. The city itself has everything that one could possibly need, but it often requires a long walk, bus or taxi to reach. Banks, post office, an excellent selection of shops plus all the facilities of a major ferry port. Tourist information office.

Hospital, doctors, dentists, and pharmacies.

Chandleries near the marina, or a couple of blocks away. Chart agents next to the yacht club. Engines, hulls, electronics and sails can be repaired. Mobile crane. Slipways within the marina area where it is possible to dry out alongside the wall for scrubbing off, or any other necessary work.

Communications

Ferries to Southampton and Dover. Railway station and bus service. Car hire and taxis. Airport.

History

Le Havre is a comparatively new harbour, having been founded in 1517 by the forward thinking French king, François I, a contemporary of the young Henry VIII of England. The harbour it replaced, Harfleur, had silted up to such an extent that it was virtually unusable. The new port, Le Havre de Grâce, to give it its full name, grew rapidly despite setbacks such as capture by the English in 1562 and bombardment by a joint Dutch and English force in 1694.

As France's second largest port after Marseille, Le Havre was heavily bombed during the Second World War. By the time the war was over there was little of the town still standing. Unlike other war-damaged towns such as Caen and St-Malo which were rebuilt in a style faithful to their past, Le Havre was rebuilt in a modern and utilitarian style. The buildings all seem to be glass and concrete, but the streets are wide and there are trees and parks to soften the austerity.

To see and do

For those who enjoy museums, art galleries, concerts and other cultural events, Le Havre has a lot to offer. The tourist office near the town hall is an excellent source of information on places to see and cultural events. In the Quartier St-François, one of the oldest parts of Le Havre which survived the war, is a museum devoted to the history of Le Havre. The Musée des Beaux Arts André Malraux, which is situated behind the signal tower in the outer harbour, has a large collection of Impressionist paintings. There is a magnificent view from the top of the octagonal tower of the church of St-Joseph (built in 1954), situated close to the marina. The coloured glass windows enliven the climb up the tower. Near to the harbour there is also a natural history museum. Some distance from the harbour is the Montgeon Forest where, amongst other attractions, is the zoo.

Fécamp

Position 49°46′N 0°22′E
Charts Admiralty 2656, 2612, 1352 (plan)
Imray C31

General

Fécamp is one of those welcoming harbours which calls you back time after time. Ashore there is so much to see that you should plan on spending several days here if you are to make the most of your visit. Fécamp is famous for its Bénédictine liqueur, and a visit to the Bénédictine museum and distillery is almost obligatory! The town however has far more to offer, most of it convenient to the marina. If a meal out is included in your plan of action take care to book a table in advance. Fécamp restaurants are particularly busy.

From a practical point of view Fécamp can be entered at most states of tide (except on LWS) and in all but strong onshore winds. It makes a convenient port of entry or departure, and duty-free goods are easily obtained. Although it is still a commercial and fishing port facilities for yachts are excellent.

Tidal information

HW is HW Dieppe −0020, HW Dover −0100.

Height of tide above chart datum
MHWS 7·9m, MHWN 6·5m, MLWN 2·6m, MLWS 0·8m

Tidal streams
The tidal streams set across the harbour entrance. The flood stream (E-going) can reach 2½ knots and is considerably stronger than the ebb. The tidal stream flowing in and out of the harbour reaches 1 knot on springs and ½ knot on neaps.
HW Fécamp −0515 E-going stream begins (2½ knots on springs)
HW Fécamp +0010 slack water
HW Fécamp +0025 W-going stream begins (weak)

Minimum depths
The harbour is dredged to 1m below chart datum. Note however that the channel is liable to silting, especially after bad weather. There is a minimum depth of 2m at the yacht club pontoon berths, and 5m inside the Bassin Bérigny.

The approach to Fécamp.

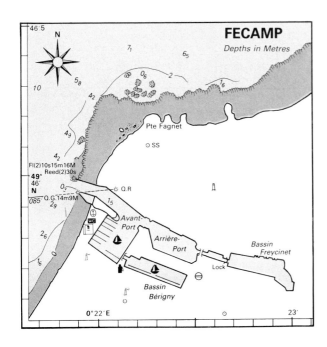

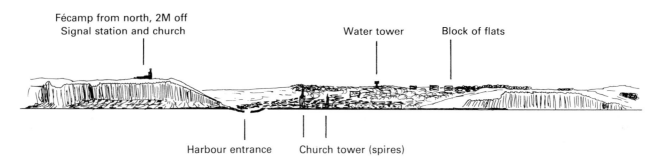

Fécamp from north, 2M off
Signal station and church · Water tower · Block of flats

Harbour entrance · Church tower (spires)

Fécamp

Timing
If you wish to lock into the Bassin Bérigny the lock gates are open from approximately 1½ to 2 hours before HW until HW.

Approach
Fécamp can be identified by the church of Notre Dame de Salut, which has a black roof, and the nearby signal station built on the cliff-top to the north of the harbour. Various towers and spires in the dip to the southwest can be seen. In the nearer approach the harbour breakwaters are apparent.

The harbour is approached on a course of 085°. Note that the north breakwater is built on the edge of a bank of rocks, so take care to keep on the correct approach course. As you close the harbour entrance aim to pass midway between the breakwater heads, thus avoiding a spit which extends off the southern breakwater. Once inside the harbour turn to starboard to enter the Avant-Port where the marina is located.

Entry to the harbour is controlled by traffic signals which are displayed at the root of the south breakwater. The simplified code is used.

In moderate onshore winds there is a strong surge in the harbour entrance, which penetrates into the Avant-Port. Entry and departure are dangerous in strong onshore winds from west to northwest, when surf breaks in the entrance.

Lights
S breakwater Q.G.14m9M In line 085° with
N breakwater (shore end) Q.R.10m (085°)
N breakwater Fl(2)10s15m16M Reed(2)30s

Port radio
VHF Ch 9.

Berth
Visitors may berth at the pontoon berths in the outer harbour (the Avant-Port) as directed by the marina staff, who will also help secure the yacht. Alternatively it is possible to lock into the Bassin Bérigny. In either case harbour dues are payable and include the use of the showers and toilets. After a stay of 48 hours the third night is free.

The entrance to Fécamp.

Shelter
Normally shelter is excellent, but in strong onshore winds swell makes the pontoon berths in the Avant-Port uncomfortable. In these circumstances the best berth is locked into the Bassin Bérigny.

Officials
The yacht club and *Capitainerie* share the same building at the head of the pontoons, ☎ 35 28 13 58. Weather forecasts are posted up at the office. The customs office is located on the Chaussée Gayant. Police in the town.

Facilities
Water and electricity are laid onto the pontoons in the Avant-Port. There is a fuel berth (petrol and diesel) near the entrance to the Bassin Bérigny. For service apply to the yacht club office. You must take a minimum of 50 litres of fuel, and it is closed Wednesdays.

Showers, toilets and a bar at the yacht club. Orders for duty-free goods can be placed at the club office. Chandlery near the yacht club.

There are a number of shops and restaurants on the quays of the Avant-Port and of the Bassin

Fécamp marina is exceptionally well organised and welcoming. The lock into the inner basin is visible in the centre left, opposite the marina berths. The fuel berth is next to the lock.

Bérigny, but the majority of the shops, supermarkets, banks, and post office are in the town centre to the east of the harbour around the church of St-Etienne. There is a large Champion hypermarket near the railway station. Open-air fruit and vegetable market on Fridays. Fresh fish is sold on the quayside. Laundrette in Rue des Forts, near the abbey church of La Trinité. The tourist information office is near the southwest corner of the Avant-Port.

There is a mobile crane. Repairs to hull and engine are possible.

Hospital, doctors, dentists, pharmacies.

Communications

Railway station and bus service. Car hire and taxis.

History

There are two possible derivations for the name of Fécamp, each of which fits in with the history of the port. Some sources say that the name comes from the Norse *fiske*, meaning fish. Indeed fishing has played an important part in the lives of the people since the earliest times, and in later centuries its fishermen sailed to distant fishing grounds off Newfoundland.

A more colourful source of the name, however, comes from the Latin, *fici campus*, meaning the field of the fig. Legend has it that a fig tree in which Joseph of Arimathea (or Nicodemus, depending on the version) had hidden a phial of Christ's blood was washed up on the shores of Fécamp. At the place where it came to rest a spring of water miraculously gushed forth. This spring now supplies the fountain of the Precious Blood, the Source du Précieux-Sang, which is still an object of piety. The phial of Holy Blood became one of the relics of the abbey which was subsequently founded at Fécamp.

Fécamp naturally became a centre of pilgrimage, and religious houses were established to cater for their needs. The original convent, founded in 663 AD, was however destroyed by marauding Vikings. A new abbey was built under the patronage of the Dukes of Normandy, descendants of the Viking raiders. When the church was being rededicated in 943 an angel turned up, conveniently leaving his footprint in the floor, and giving instructions that the church was to be dedicated to the Holy Trinity. This footprint is said to be near the altar in the south transept, but is far from obvious.

In 1001 William of Dijon, who had reformed the abbey at Cluny, was invited to Fécamp by Richard I to take the abbey in hand. Fécamp became the most important centre of pilgrimage in Normandy before the development of Mont-St-Michel.

Besides being a religious centre Fécamp was once the capital of Normandy. Its political importance only declined when the interests of the Dukes of Normandy switched to England. The ruins of the ducal palace can be seen opposite the church of the Holy Trinity.

Today Fécamp is famous as the place where the liqueur Bénédictine is distilled. The liqueur is said to have been developed by a monk called Vincelli in 1510. The secret recipe was rediscovered by the entrepreneur, Alexander Le Grand, in the nineteenth century. Le Grand was a skilled promoter of his elixir and became very wealthy. He commissioned an elaborate mock Gothic and Renaissance building to house his collection of priceless artifacts, many of which had come from the Bénédictine abbey.

To see

To make the most of a visit to Fécamp it is worth obtaining a map from the tourist information office showing all the principal sights of interest. Chief amongst these are the Bénédictine museum and distillery, the former abbey church of La Trinité which houses the relic of the Holy Blood and the tombs of Dukes Richard I and Richard II of Normandy, the Fountain of the Holy Blood, and the municipal museum. Do not miss visiting the church of La Trinité. It is one of the most breathtakingly beautiful churches in Normandy.

As a change from sightseeing Fécamp can offer a choice of recreational facilities. These include a swimming pool, tennis courts, riding, way-marked paths, a theatre and a casino.

St-Valéry-en-Caux

Position 49°52′N 0°43′E
Charts Admiralty *2612*
      Imray *C31*

General

This small and charming holiday town hidden in a valley between chalk cliffs, has a harbour containing an unbelievable 600 yacht berths. The town consists mainly of modern buildings, softened by memorable displays of flowers. The historic town centre was largely destroyed in the early part of the Second World War when it was the scene of the last stand of the 51st Highland Division and the 2nd French Cavalry Division against the Nazis.

Despite St-Valéry's modern character this is an attractive harbour, and in good conditions is an idyllic port of call.

Tidal information

HW is HW Dieppe −0016, Dover −0046.

Height of tide above chart datum
MHWS 8·9m, MHWN 7·1m, MLWN 2·5m, MLWS 1·0m

Tidal streams
The tidal streams at St-Valéry-en-Caux run strongly across the entrance, up to 2½ knots on the flood and 2 knots on the ebb. The flood starts ½ an hour after LW Dieppe, and the ebb starts to flow at HW.

Tidal streams setting across the entrance are complicated on the flood by a countercurrent which, from a point east of the entrance, flows seaward along the east breakwater. Part of this eddy then runs into the harbour, whilst part sets west across the entrance.

Minimum depths
The outer harbour dries out completely and the approach channel dries out for 1 cable to seaward of the breakwaters. On HW springs there is a depth of 4·5m in the harbour. On neaps the depth is 3m. Entry is possible in good weather for a moderate draught yacht from half tide.

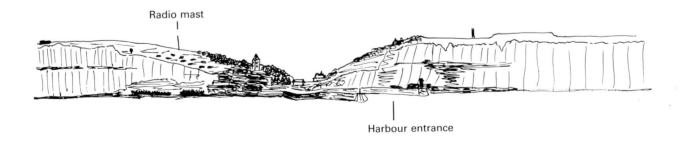

Radio mast

Harbour entrance

St-Valéry-en-Caux from north, 1M off.

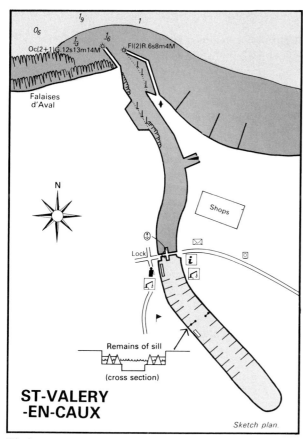

Falaises
d'Aval

Oc(2+1)G.12s13m14M

Fl(2)R.6s8m4M

Shops

Lock

Remains of sill

(cross section)

**ST-VALERY
-EN-CAUX**

Sketch plan.

The lock and road bridge are open, allowing entry to the inner basin at St-Valéry-en-Caux. The old timber-framed house on the right-hand side was one of the few medieval buildings in St-Valéry to survive the last war.

The inner basin at St-Valéry-en-Caux, looking towards the lock and the opening bridge.

Timing

The lock into the inner harbour is open from approximately 2¼ hours before HW to 2¼ hours after HW, depending on the height of the tide. The exact times are posted up at the lock-keeper's office. The road bridge across the lock opens on the hour and on the half hour.

Lights, using the simplified code, control entry to and departure from the inner basin. R and G together prohibit all movement; R permits exit only from the basin; G allows entry only to the inner basin.

Approach

St-Valéry-en-Caux can be difficult to find from seaward, since it nestles in a narrow valley and the houses are hidden by the chalk cliffs. There is however a R and W radio mast just east of the town and a large white building overlooking the town on the eastern side. In the nearer approach the breakwaters, with a white lighthouse on the head of the west one, can be discerned.

Once identified the harbour can be approached from the northeast. Note that approximately 8 cables east-northeast of the harbour entrance there is an area with just 0·6m over it. If there is insufficient water to enter and it is calm, anchor in mud (good holding) to seaward of the entrance.

Enter on a southwest course keeping closer to the east breakwater. Inside the breakwaters a bank builds up on the west side of the channel, so keep well over towards the piles marking the east side.

Once inside the Avant-Port there are a number of buoys to which you can moor whilst waiting for the lock to open.

Lights

W breakwater Oc(2+1)G.12s13m14M
E breakwater Fl(2)R.6s8m4M

Port radio

VHF Ch 9.

Berth

As you pass through the lock the lock-keeper will direct you to a berth. Visitors normally berth alongside the pontoon on the starboard side, just beyond the lock, but you may be directed to a finger berth further in. Note that berthing or departing can be tricky because of strong currents within the Bassin à Flot when the lock gates are open.

Shelter

Although the outer harbour is exposed to considerable surge in strong onshore winds the inner harbour provides excellent shelter when the lock gates are closed.

Officials

The lock-keeper collects harbour dues and is a good source of information, ☎ 35 97 01 30. Weather forecasts and lock opening times are posted up at his office. Police in the town. The customs office has been closed down, the nearest one is at Fécamp. The yacht club is located on the west side of the Bassin à Flot.

Facilities

Water is supplied to the pontoons which lie at 90° to the quays. There is no water on the visitors' pontoon. Electricity sockets are on the quaysides above the pontoons, and long cables are required. Fuel is available from a garage across the road on the Quai du Havre. *Camping Gaz* is sold in the town. There is a shower block in the building between the sailing club and the bar. Showers are available between 0830 and 2030 at a cost of about 8fr., payable at the bar.

In the town and close to the harbour there is a reasonable selection of shops, including a well stocked supermarket, a hardware shop and a chandlery. On Fridays there is an excellent open-air fruit and vegetable market in the square near the town hall. Fresh fish is sold daily on the quayside. In addition there are banks, post office, and a tourist information office. The laundrette is at 10 Rue de Dieppe, conveniently close to the harbour.

Doctors, dentists, hospital, and pharmacy. Hotels and restaurants.

Communications

Railway station, bus service, taxis, car and bicycle hire.

History

In the seventh century St-Valéry founded a monastery here amongst the chalk landscape, hence the town's name (*caux* means chalk). A village of fishermen soon grew up around the monastery. With the discovery of Newfoundland and Iceland towards the end of the fifteenth century St-Valéry fishermen were amongst the first to exploit the rich fishing grounds in search of cod. Their vessels were built locally.

During the French Wars of Religion Henry IV came to St-Valéry-en-Caux and is reputed to have stayed at the old timber-framed house, which stands on the west side of the Avant-Port. This house is currently being restored.

In 1940 part of the British Tenth Army retreated before the Nazis to St-Valéry-en-Caux. The 51st Highland Division and the 2nd French Cavalry Division together bravely resisted the Nazi Panzers, and only surrendered after heavy losses and the destruction of the central part of the town. The Allied surrender was accepted by Erwin Rommel.

To see and do

St-Valéry-en-Caux is proud of the sixteenth-century house where Henry IV slept, one of the few old buildings to survive the destruction of 1940. Up a narrow twisting road to the west of the harbour there is a fine cloister in the Hospice des Pénitents which dates from 1640.

There are three monuments at St-Valéry-en-Caux which can be reached on foot. On the heights to the west of the Avant-Port there is the memorial to the French troops who lost their lives in the defence of St-Valéry in 1940. On the cliffs to the east of the town are two memorials, one to the 51st Highland Division and one to the aviators Coste and Bellonte. In 1930 Coste and Bellonte successfully completed the first flight from France to America in an aircraft named *Pointe d'Interrogation* ('question mark').

Being a holiday resort St-Valéry is well equipped with recreational facilities. These include a heated swimming pool, tennis courts, sailboard hire, a casino with a theatre and cinema.

Dieppe

Position 49°56′N 1°05′E
Charts Admiralty *2612, 2147*
Imray *C31*

General

The harbour of Dieppe is primarily a ferry terminal and fishing port with only basic provision for yachts. Yachts, staying as temporary members of the Cercle de la Voile de Dieppe, share the Bassin Duquesne with the fishing fleet. Both the outer and inner harbours are typical of fishing ports; smelly and extremely dirty, with an uncomfortable surge. One can only admire the dedication of the local yachtsmen!

To set against these disadvantages the yacht club is one of the friendliest we have visited, and the town, which is delightful, is just a stone's throw from the yacht club.

As you would expect of a busy ferry port the harbour can be entered at any state of tide. It is, however, dangerous to enter in strong onshore winds from northwest to northeast.

Tidal information

Dieppe is a standard port. HW is HW Dover −0030.

Height of tide above chart datum
MHWS 9·3m, MHWN 7·2m, MLWN 2·6m, MLWS 0·7m

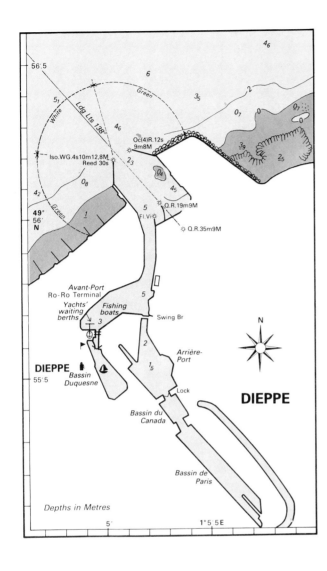

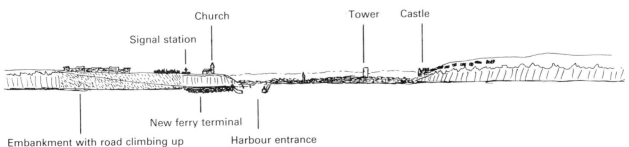

Minimum depths

The harbour and entrance are dredged to 3·5m. Some areas within the tidal parts of the harbour dry.

Timing

Depending on weather conditions most yachts can enter the harbour at any state of tide. Access to the yacht berths in the Basin Duquesne, however, is only possible when the lock is open from 2 hours before HW to 1 hour after HW.

Approach

There are no offlying dangers in the immediate approach to Dieppe. The seabed, however, is uneven and in bad weather you can expect particularly rough seas.

Dieppe lies approximately 5 miles east of Pointe d'Ailly. The lighthouse at Pointe d'Ailly is a low squat building surrounded by trees and, in daylight, not immediately conspicuous.

Dieppe lies in a cleft in the chalk cliffs, where the river Arques enters the sea. It can be identified by a conspicuous church with a spire built on the cliff top above the harbour entrance and to the east of the town. There is also a prominent signal station near the church. On the opposite side of the town, on the slopes above it, stands the castle which further aids positive identification.

The harbour entrance is easily distinguished in the nearer approach. Once the entrance has been identified a course of 138° leads into the harbour. At night leading lights are displayed.

Beware of a strong current setting across the harbour entrance, and of unlit buoys and nets set out in the bay.

Entry can be difficult in strong winds with any north in them. Strong northerly winds produce dangerous seas at the entrance.

Traffic control signals, using the full code, are displayed from a mast on the west breakwater. Additional signals which may be shown are a W light above and to the left of the traffic signals, indicating that the lock gates are open, and a R or G light above and to the right of the traffic signals, indicating that a ferry is entering (G) or leaving (R). Two R lights above and to the right of the traffic signals indicate that a dredger is working in the harbour.

Tidal streams

Off the harbour entrance:

Local HW −0500 E-going flood starts (maximum rate 2 knots).

Local HW +0040 W-going ebb starts (maximum rate 1½ knots).

Dieppe from 1½M north.

The entrance to Dieppe, viewed from northeast.

Arethusa leaving Dieppe.

In poor visibility entry is prohibited when the fog signal on the west breakwater gives a blast of 1s every 5s.

When the traffic control signals are lit yachts must keep out of the way and it is imperative that they also obey these signals. The reason for this becomes apparent when you enter. There are a number of blind bends which could easily hide a ferry, and passing room is limited.

Lights

Pointe d'Ailly Fl(3)20s95m31M RC
W breakwater Iso.WG.4s10m12/8M Reed 30s
E breakwater Oc(4)R.12s19m8M
Leading lights 138° Q.R.19m9M and Q.R.35m9M

Radiobeacon

Pointe d'Ailly Lt *AL* 310·3 kHz 50M Seq 4 Cont
49°55′N 0°57′·55E

Port radio

VHF Ch 12.

Dieppe Avant-Port. The lifting bridge spans the lock to the Bassin Duquesne. Yachts can wait for the tide at the pontoon opposite the ferry.

Berth

On entering follow the harbour (the Avant-Port) around to starboard. The car ferries berth alongside the north wall of this tidal basin. In the southwest corner is a lock and lifting road bridge with the control tower to the west. The yacht berths are beyond the lock in the Bassin Duquesne. The lock gates open from 2 hours before HW until 1 hour after HW. In theory the lifting bridge opens on demand (two long blasts on your horn), but you may have to wait. Note that the simplified code of traffic signals regulates entry to and departure from the Bassin Duquesne.

If the lock is closed tie up temporarily at the waiting pontoon near the control tower. It is not advisable to leave the boat unattended here, because of the surge and fishing boat and ferry activity. Once through the lock gates you are in the Bassin Duquesne. Yachts of up to 15m in length berth on the west and northwest sides, often 3 abreast, alongside very low floating pontoons. If there is room the best berth is in the far northwest corner, tucked behind the wall and sheltered from the surge caused by

Fishing boats share the Bassin Duquesne in Dieppe with yachts. The yachts in the background tucked behind the spur are sheltered from the fishing-boat wash.

fishing boats. Unfortunately this is where all the flotsam seems to pile up. The wake from passing fishing boats can be a real problem if you are tied up opposite the fish quay. Unless you are well fendered you could suffer damage.

Shelter

The inner harbour, the Bassin Duquesne, offers excellent shelter, but a surge enters the tidal basins in onshore winds.

Officials

The yacht club, housed in the small white-painted wooden building, administers the berths in the inner basin. The club officials are helpful and able to provide advice, ☎ 35 84 32 99. The customs office is nearby on the corner of Rue de Général de Gaulle and Rue Descroizilles. Police in the town.

Harbour dues

The yacht club issues temporary membership cards, and it charges by the night. During the summer months the maximum number of nights you can spend here is 8.

Weather forecasts

The weather forecast is posted up at the yacht club.

Facilities

Water from the taps on the quaysides above the yacht club pontoons. No electricity. Fuel from a filling station about 5 minutes walk from the yacht club in the Rue de Général de Gaulle (see plan). Showers are available at the yacht club between 0830 and 1900 hours at a cost of about 5fr. The yacht club also has a bar.

There is a full range of shops in Dieppe, most of which are within easy walking distance of the boat. The hypermarket is on the outskirts of town, on the road to Rouen, and can be reached by bus. The main market is on Saturday mornings when it overflows from the square outside the church of St-Jacques into the Grande Rue. Other market days are Tuesdays and Thursdays. Daily fish market. Duty-free stores can be obtained. There is a chandlery on the Quai du Carénage.

A number of banks, the post office and the tourist information office are close at hand. The laundrette is at 44-46 Rue de l'Epée, to the north of the Grande Rue.

Repairs to engine, hull, sails and electronic equipment can be carried out locally.

There is an excellent choice of restaurants, mainly specialising in fish dishes.

Hospital, doctors, dentists, and pharmacies.

Communications

Ferries to Newhaven. Railway station and bus service. Car hire and taxis.

To do

Dieppe is a popular holiday resort as well as a ferry port and there is no shortage of entertainment and recreational facilities. There is a heated swimming pool if the sea is too cold for you, a thalassic therapy centre, tennis courts, crazy golf, casino, children's playground, and a fair.

The castle, on a slope overlooking the town, was built in the fifteenth century to defend the town against English raiders. It now houses a museum and is well worth visiting. The museum has a fabulous collection of carved ivories for which Dieppe is famous, as well as a maritime section and paintings by famous artists such as Monet, Dufy, Pissarro and Braque. The church of St-Jacques, currently being restored, has some fine Gothic sculpture. Inside the church is a useful chart in English outlining the history of Dieppe itself as well as that of the church. In the square outside the church is a statue of the famous French explorer and seaman, Champlain. Les Tourelles, a sixteenth-century gateway to the old town, overlooks the beach.

History

The people of Dieppe have over the centuries looked to the sea for their livelihood. The deep water at the mouth of the river Arques gave them an unrivalled advantage over many other harbours. The town's name is in fact said to be derived from the old English 'doep', or from a similar Norse word, meaning 'deep'.

Initially it seems that fishing was the harbour's main activity and that Dieppe was a minor port, but after William the Conqueror became king of England Dieppe grew increasingly important. The connection with England was not however always to Dieppe's advantage. In 1195 the town was attacked and burnt by the French king, Philippe-August, in his war against Richard the Lionheart. English rule ended in 1204 when Dieppe, with the rest of Normandy, was annexed by the French crown.

Dieppe's seamen were both adventurous and enterprising, and contributed to the wealth of the port. They travelled far and wide, discovering new lands, founding colonies, and bringing back spices and ivory, amongst other goods. The ivory was fashioned into some of the most exquisite objects, examples of which are exhibited in the castle museum. Amongst the most notable of Dieppe's seamen were the men who in 1364 founded a small colony called Petit Dieppe in Sierra Leone. Other notable men were Aubert who discovered Newfoundland, Verrazano (a Florentine who lived in Dieppe) who discovered the east coast of the United States of America and the bay of New York, and Jean and Raoul Parmentier who discovered the Molucca islands.

In the seventeenth century the emphasis switched to colonisation and Dieppe men were again in the forefront. Ribault founded a colony in Florida and Diel d'Enambuc founded colonies in Martinique and Guadeloupe. The most famous coloniser was however Samuel Champlain who colonised Canada. The town also bred its fair share of pirates who preyed on English shipping.

Trade flourished with Dieppe vessels regularly sailing to Africa and Brazil. Dieppe merchants and ship owners such as Jehan Anjo became rich and powerful. Anjo was so wealthy that he entertained the king, François I, and was able to lend him vast sums of money. He also waged a private war against the Portuguese in 1524 which he won.

In 1694 Dieppe was bombarded by a joint Anglo-Dutch fleet. Most of the houses were built of carved wood, and in the resulting fire 90% of the town was burnt to the ground. The town was rebuilt over a period of 25 years by one of Vauban's engineers, Ventabren. Vauban was not over-impressed with Ventabren's efforts.

During the nineteenth century Dieppe was discovered by the Duchess de Berry who promoted it as a fashionable bathing resort. It was patronised by the English as well as by Parisians.

In 1942 Dieppe was the scene of a trial invasion of France by the Allies, the so-called Dieppe Raid. Dieppe was so well defended by the Nazis that the attack was repulsed with heavy losses. 68% of the Canadian troops and 20% of the British commandos were killed, injured or taken prisoner. The Dieppe Raid, although unsuccessful, taught the Allies a number of lessons which were put to good use in the invasion of Normandy in 1944.

Le Tréport

Position 50°04′N 1°22′E
Charts Admiralty *2147, 1352* (plan)
Imray *C31*

General

The small commercial and fishing port of Le Tréport lies at the mouth of the river Bresle, and is flanked on either side by spectacular white chalk cliffs which are claimed to be the highest in Europe. Le Tréport lies on the south side of the river, whilst its neighbour, Mers-les-Bains, lies on the north side. Both towns are busy holiday resorts with all that that entails. The harbour however has a more sober purpose. It boasts a small but active fishing fleet, and an inner basin equipped with wharves and cranes for the use of small coasters. Unfortunately the only berths suitable for visiting yachts are in the commercial wet dock, where the surroundings are far from salubrious.

In the right conditions however a stay at Le Tréport can be pleasant, and it is a convenient base from which to visit Eu.

Tidal information

HW is Dieppe +0005, Dover −0025

Height of tide above chart datum
MHWS 9·4m, MHWN 7·4m, MLWN 2·5m, MLWS 0·7m

Tidal streams
At the harbour entrance the tidal streams flow as follows, reaching a maximum rate of 1 knot at springs:
HW Dieppe −0600 E-going flood starts
HW Dieppe W-going ebb starts

Minimum depths
The harbour entrance dries out completely (2m above chart datum) at LW, but most yachts should be able to enter 2 or 3 hours either side of HW, in good weather.

Timing
The lock between the Avant-Port and the Arrière-Port opens approximately 1½ hours before HW, although this can vary depending on the weather and height of the tide. It closes on HW. There is a pedestrian bridge at the lock which will open on request (three blasts of the horn).

Approach

Le Tréport is easy to identify positively. The high cliffs on either side of a wide valley with an obviously sizeable town fronting the shore on the low land are distinctive. Further to the northeast the high cliffs start to give way to the low land around the Somme estuary. In the centre of the cluster of buildings a square factory painted with broad red and white bands and with a squat square chimney to

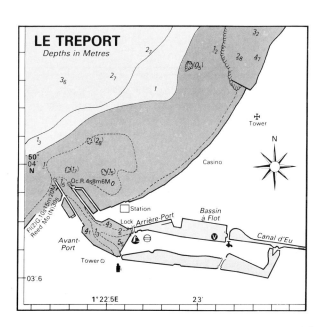

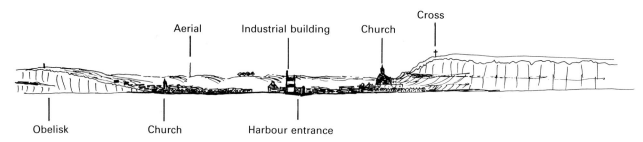

Aerial Industrial building Church Cross

Obelisk Church Harbour entrance

Le Tréport from 2M northwest.

Small fishing boats can enter Le Tréport from half tide.

one side is conspicuous. Closer in the church to the south of the harbour becomes obvious, as do the cross (illuminated at night) on the cliff top to the southwest of the town, the scar of the disused funicular railway in the cliff below the cross, and the pillar on top of a hill close to the northeast.

The dangers in the approach to Le Tréport are the Ridins du Tréport which is a shoal patch (4·9m) lying 2¾ miles northwest of the harbour entrance, and, more importantly, two drying rocks located 6 and 3½ cables to the west of the harbour entrance, 3½ cables offshore.

Keep at least ½ mile offshore until the harbour entrance bears between 112° and 120°. It is then possible to steer for the harbour entrance, but beware of a strong tidal set across the approach channel and entrance. Do not attempt to enter in strong onshore winds.

Lights
W breakwater Fl(2)G.10s15m20M Reed Mo(N)30s
E breakwater Oc.R.4s8m6M

Port radio
VHF Ch 12.

Berth
Once through the breakwaters you are in the Avant-Port, which is used by the fishing boats, and a few small motorboats and yachts which are kept on drying moorings on the north side. The entrance to the Arrière-Port lies beyond these moorings in the far east corner.

Two buoys (unlit) on the starboard hand mark a shoal area. If the pedestrian bridge across the entrance is closed it will open on request. Once

A panoramic view of the harbour, Le Tréport and Mer-les-Bains.

through you come to the Arrière-Port. In the far corner on the port-hand side there is a pontoon for the use of the few local yachts. Visitors should proceed into the next basin (the Bassin à Flot) and tie up alongside the quay at the far east end. This is a long way from the town and lacking in security, but there is a water tap nearby. Yachts are permitted to stay for up to 48 hours.

If you miss the lock it may be possible to tie up alongside the quay on the south side of the Avant-Port, but you will be in the way of the fishing boats and not particularly welcome.

Shelter
A strong surge enters the outer, drying sections, of the harbour in onshore winds. Within the Bassin à Flot there is good shelter.

Officials
The white building near the lock, formerly the harbourmaster's office, is no longer used as such. Information can be obtained at the lock operators' office, the small modern brick building. The customs office is on the Quai Edouard Gelée. Police in both Le Tréport and Mers-les-Bains. Harbourmaster ☎ 35 86 17 91.

Harbour dues
Visiting yachts may still not be charged for short visits.

Facilities
Water tap on the quay in the far southeast corner of the Bassin à Flot. Fuel can be obtained from a filling station near the southeast corner of the Avant-Port. The berth in the Bassin à Flot is out of the way, but most needs can be met by either walking to Le Tréport or Mers-les-Bains. Both towns have post offices, banks, and a reasonable selection of shops. There is a Mammouth hypermarket on the outskirts of Mers-les-Bains, served by bus. The bus timetable is available from the tourist information office. There is an open-air fruit and vegetable market in the Place de l'Eglise in Le Tréport on Tuesday and Saturday mornings. Fish market. Le Tréport tourist information office is in the casino building near the beach. In Mers-les-Bains the tourist information office is in the town hall. Doctors and dentists. Restaurants.

Limited mechanical repairs are possible at various garages or at Atelier Coopératif, 9 Rue des Salines. For other repairs obtain advice from Manureva Sport, 61 Quai François 1er, or from Loisirs Yachting, 4 Av. des Canadiens.

Communications

Railway station on the north side of the Avant-Port. Bus service, taxis and car hire. There is an airport at Eu.

History

The name of Le Tréport comes from the Latin, Ulterioris Portus, which denoted its function as the sea (or lower) port for the Roman colony. The town of Eu, further upstream, was the colony's river (or upper) port.

In the ninth and tenth centuries life would have been particularly arduous for the inhabitants of Le Tréport because of frequent Viking raids. Le Tréport was an obvious landing point for Viking raiders who, after a bit of local rape and pillage, could continue upriver to plunder settlements further inland.

In 1036 Robert, Count of Eu, founded the abbey of Saint Michel at Le Tréport. The foundation of the abbey led to increased status for the town, and economic growth. The abbey was destroyed during the French Revolution.

The Hundred Years War brought hard times and destruction to Le Tréport, and a plague also decimated the population. Despite these problems Le Tréport continued to grow and flourish as a port. It handled wines from Gascony and Aquitaine, and exported salt from its saltpans, and wood from the forest of Eu. In the twelfth century the river changed its course and started to silt up. As a result Le Tréport began to lose trade to Dieppe. The decline was only reversed in 1773 when the Duke of Penthièvre, who was also count of Eu, funded the construction of a lock. In the following century the harbour was further improved and a canal leading to Eu was built. Unfortunately this canal is no longer in use.

Queen Victoria landed at Le Tréport in 1843 when she went to stay with king Louis-Philippe at his summer palace in Eu. She was so impressed with Normandy and Louis-Philippe's hospitality that she returned again in 1845.

It was during the nineteenth century that Le Tréport developed as a sea bathing resort, visitors initially arriving by coach. With the construction and opening of the railway in 1872 the influx of visitors increased to such an extent that there was insufficient accommodation for them in Le Tréport. The visitors therefore turned to the small village of Mers-les-Bains which soon grew.

Le Tréport with its prominent church.

To see and do

Both resorts have heated swimming pools and casinos. Tennis and mini golf are also on offer. There are walks to the tops of the cliffs, from which there are splendid views over the harbour. Unfortunately you have to climb them under your own steam as the funicular railway at Le Tréport has been closed.

The sixteenth-century church of St-Jacques at Le Tréport was built using different types of stones and flints, creating an attractive pattern.

The historic town of Eu lies about 3 miles inland, and can be reached by bus. It is an attractive little town, full of traditional shops, and with a palace set in fine formal gardens. The palace houses a museum with furniture and examples of local crafts. Eu's great claim to fame is that it was here that William the Conqueror married his cousin, Matilda of Flanders. The Pope disapproved of the marriage because he considered that they were too closely related, and excommunicated them. The excommunication was only lifted when William and Matilda repented, and as penance each built an abbey in Caen.

The Somme Estuary

General

Looking at the charts and reading the Admiralty pilot the shallow waters of the Somme estuary do not seem at all inviting. Do not be put off however. This is one of the most attractive and least spoilt areas along this coast, and a rewarding cruising ground. You do need good weather to enter or leave, but if you are caught inside with bad weather you have a choice of three ports to visit, you can sail within the estuary, and ashore you will find plenty to do. You can even go up to Abbeville along the canal, without taking your mast down.

The wide bay of the Somme estuary is shallow, full of shifting sandbanks, and backed by a low sandy coastline. In bad weather the seas break on banks to seaward of the bay. The three ports in the estuary are Le Hourdel, Le Crotoy and St-Valéry-sur-Somme. All three are fishing harbours.

Le Hourdel is a tiny hamlet, decidedly lacking in facilities, but where the majority of the Somme fishing fleet seems to berth. The channel to Le Hourdel is not marked, and once there it is next to impossible to tie up alongside the quay for all the fishing boats. Le Hourdel would therefore only appeal to yachtsmen who would be happy to dry out at the top of the creek, and who do not look for any shore facilities.

Le Crotoy is an odd little place, where tourism is growing. It is a mixture of simple single-storey cottages, reminiscent of some villages in Fife, together with more elaborate villas and houses. Beyond the fish quay on the outskirts of town is a new harbour

where the Club Nautique de la Baie de Somme has its own pontoon berths. Le Crotoy boasts the only south-facing beach on the north coast of France.

St-Valéry-sur-Somme is the main port in the estuary. It has excellent facilities for visiting yachts at the yacht club, the Sport Nautique Valericain, and visitors are made most welcome. The approach to St-Valéry is straightforward, and once moored at the yacht club there are plenty of attractions ashore. It is at St-Valéry that you can enter the Canal de la Somme, and hence the network of canals which traverse France. Yachts can proceed as far as Abbeville without taking their masts down. With the mast lowered yachts can reach Paris, the Rhine, or the Mediterranean.

Charts Admiralty *2612*
Imray *C31*

Up-to-date charts of the estuary are not available because of the constantly shifting sandbanks. The channels are however well marked, and, in good visibility, straightforward to follow. You could write to the yacht club at St-Valéry for a plan of the buoyage, but by the time you arrive the situation could have changed and your information be misleading.

Tidal streams

At the entrance to the bay tidal streams are strongest as the banks cover and uncover.
HW Dieppe −0400 flood begins
HW Dieppe −0130 maximum flood (3kn springs) – direction NE
HW Dieppe +0200 ebb begins
HW Dieppe +0500 maximum ebb (3kn springs) – direction SW

Minimum depths

Small coasters, drawing up to 3·4m, can reach St-Valéry on spring tides, so it is unlikely that a yacht will be too deep to navigate the estuary. On neap tides yachts drawing up to 1·4m should find ample water. Le Crotoy can be reached with a 2m draught on springs, and perhaps 1m on neaps. Note that the only suitable places for a fin-keeled yacht are in the marinas at St-Valéry, where some berths have 2m at LW and Le Crotoy, where some berths have 1m at LW. Alternatively it is possible to dry out alongside the quay at St-Valéry.

Approach

The low-lying ground around the Somme estuary means that it is not easily identified from seaward. Coming from the direction of Le Tréport the cliffs give way at Ault to low hills, then sand dunes. The tall white lighthouses of Cayeux-sur-Mer, located in the small village of Brighton 1¼ miles NNE of Cayeux (50°12′N 1°31′E), and Le Hourdel show up well in moderate visibility and are an aid to identification.

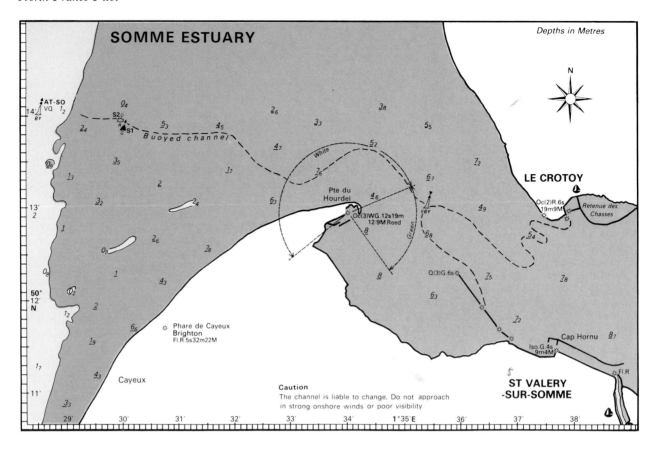

The Somme estuary dries out, and entry should only be attempted between 2 hours and 1½ hours before HW. It is not wise to approach this coast in poor visibility, and entry and departure at night are difficult, if not impossible.

Beware of the possibility that depths may be less than charted, and of a tidal set in and out of the estuary.

A lit north cardinal buoy painted *ATSO* marks the seaward edge of the drying banks. Having located the north cardinal buoy it should be possible to locate the first Somme channel buoys approximately east-southeast of the north cardinal buoy. The first buoys are *S1* and *S2*. The first starboard-hand buoy is lit. A few other buoys are lit, but these are not necessarily at the points where the channel changes direction. The stranger should not be tempted to enter at night.

The exact course of the channel is constantly changing, and the buoys are moved accordingly. It is wise however to keep an eye on your echo sounder, particularly if following the channels to Le Crotoy or Le Hourdel. The tide sets across the channel. This is most noticeable when following the channel to Le Crotoy.

The main channel leads to St-Valéry. A minor channel, marked by smaller R and G buoys (prefix *C*) leads to Le Crotoy. It leaves the main channel at a west cardinal buoy situated between buoys *30* and *32*. The channel to Le Hourdel is not marked, but it parts from the main channel at buoy *33*.

Approach in onshore winds is best avoided since the Admiralty pilot warns of the danger of any vessel grounded on the shifting sand being capsized. The fine sand washes away from the leeward side, rolling the boat. This may sound an exaggeration, but the tidal currents within the estuary run extremely strongly. Anchoring among the sands of the estuary is not advised either, since the same sand makes for poor holding!

Entry or departure at night is dangerous. It is easy to find you are out of the channel – we speak from experience here! On two occasions we tried to leave St-Valéry at night, the second time following a fishing boat. Each time we lost the channel, within a short distance of St-Valéry, and were lucky not to run aground. The problem is the distance between beacons or buoys, a strong tide setting across the channel, and very few lights.

Fishing boats trawl within the channel, and have a tendency to change course with no warning. Local yachts sail outside of the channels, but they have local knowledge or lifting keels, so it is wise not to copy them.

Lights

Ault Oc(3)WR.12s95m18/14M
Brighton (Cayeux) Fl.R.5s32m22M
Le Hourdel Oc(3)WG.12s19m12/9M Reed(3)30s
Le Crotoy Oc(2)R.6s19m9M

St-Valéry-sur-Somme yacht club pontoons and the lock into the Canal de la Somme (looking upstream).

The narrow-gauge railway of the Somme picks up passengers on the quay at St-Valéry.

N Card buoy, *ATSO* VQ, approach to the Somme
Training wall approach to St-Valéry Q(3)G.6s2m2M
Cap Hornu Iso.G.4s9m9M
St-Valéry mole Fl.R.4s9m9M

Le Hourdel

Position 50°13′N 1°34′E

Tidal information
See under St-Valéry.

Height of tide above chart datum
MHWS 10m, MHWN 7·9m

Approach
The channel to Le Hourdel is not marked and is only accessible near HW.

Berth
There is little room here for a visiting yacht. The fishing quay is busy and the only solution would be to anchor among the moorings beyond the fish quay. Since the tide is out most of the time, reaching the shore through the mud would be a problem.

Fishing vessels dried out at Le Hourdel. There is no space along-side the quay for visiting yachts. Visitors have to anchor up-stream of the quay, near the moorings.

Facilities

Water tap on the quay. Hotel with a restaurant. Café and bar. Telephone. Weather forecasts are posted up at the lighthouse.

To see

If you do not mind walking there is a famous wild-fowl reserve in the vicinity of Le Hourdel. Walk up the lane and you will find it on the other side of the main road.

Le Crotoy

Position 50°13′N 1°38′E

Tidal information

See under St-Valéry.

Approach

After leaving the main channel the channel up to Le Crotoy zig-zags across the bay. It is narrow, and it is important to follow the buoys closely. The current is strong, sets across the channel, and so demands extra concentration from the helmsman. Once you reach the fishing quay you will see the yacht masts beyond. Beware of the small buoy on the starboard-hand side of the channel which marks a shallow spit.

Berth

Within the harbour are three pontoons belonging to the local sailing club. The deepest water lies at the shoreward end of each pontoon, where three sluices wash the silt away. The water pouring through the sluices comes out with such force that the yachts nearest lean over at an angle of 30°. For a quiet night the best berth is near the outer ends of the pontoons. Tie up where space permits. There may be a club member in evidence who will give advice, but the clubhouse may be closed. You will need to obtain a key for the gates at the landward end of the pontoons.

Shelter

The harbour enjoys good all round shelter.

Officials

Harbourmaster. Police in the town. Yacht club.

Facilities

Water from the clubhouse. Fuel from garages in the town. Bank, post office and all the basic shops. Fresh fish sold daily on the quayside. Open-air fruit and vegetable market on Friday mornings in the square near the fish quay, and during the summer on Tuesday mornings in the Rue de la République. Small hull repairs can be carried out by Baie Nautique, who are to be found in the Avenue des Ecluses. Mechanical repairs are also possible. Doctor, dentist, pharmacy. Restaurants and bars.

Communications

Bus service. Taxis. Bicycle hire from the Garage de l'Avenir, 2 Rue de la Porte en Pont. A narrow gauge steam railway operates in the summer.

History

In the Middle Ages Le Crotoy was of sufficient strategic importance to have a castle built overlooking the bay. It was to this castle that Joan of Arc was brought in November 1430. She was held a prisoner in Le Crotoy for a month before being

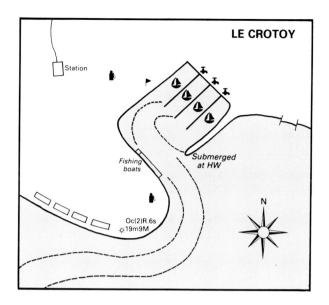

taken across the bay on foot to St-Valéry-sur-Somme. From St-Valéry her subsequent journey continued to Rouen and her martyrdom at the stake.

The castle at Le Crotoy was demolished on the king's orders in 1674. Today there is just a tiny corner of the outer wall remaining, near the beach.

After the destruction of the castle Le Crotoy's importance declined. The local inhabitants were largely dependent on fishing for a livelihood. In the nineteenth century, with the growing popularity of sea-bathing, Le Crotoy started to attract holidaymakers. Jules Verne lived at Le Crotoy from 1865 to 1870, and it was whilst he was living here that he wrote *20,000 Leagues under the Sea*.

To see and do

The narrow gauge steam railway runs from Le Crotoy around the Somme to St-Valéry, and on to Cayeux-sur-Mer. Other diversions include tennis, riding, mini-golf, sand yachting, a casino, and a fine sandy beach.

St-Valéry-sur-Somme

Position 50°11′N 1°38′E

Tidal information

Standard port Dieppe. HW St-Valéry is HW Dieppe +0035.

Height of tide above chart datum
MHWS 10m, MHWN 8m, MLWN2·5m, MLWS 0·7m

Port radio

VHF Ch 9.

Berth

The final approach channel to St-Valéry is marked by beacons mounted on training walls. The harbour entrance lies between the south bank and a mole. The most convenient and secure berth will be found at the yacht club pontoons which lie beyond the town quay. Tie up temporarily and seek guidance on a berth at the office. Most berths are bow-to the pontoons, with lines to a stern buoy. Yachts drawing less than 2m will stay afloat. There are also some berths alongside the inner pontoons, but these dry. The strong current from the direction of the canal can make berthing tricky. Before leaving the yacht club premises to explore the town make sure you have the access code for the keypad (obtainable on paying the mooring fees).

Another possibility at St-Valéry is to tie up alongside the town quay, although before leaving the boat check you are not in the normal berth of a fishing boat. Vessels moored here will take the ground.

Entering the canal system

The lock leading into the Canal de la Somme is beyond the yacht club berths. The lock is operated for a short time at the top of the tide. It is advisable

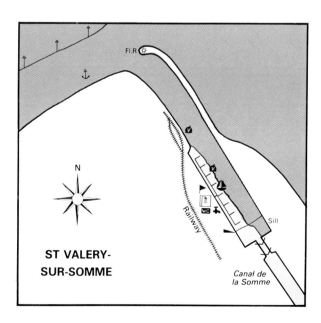

Fishing boats moored alongside the town quay at St-Valéry-sur-Somme.

to seek guidance on the current procedures at the yacht club or telephone the lock-keeper on ☎ 22 60 80 23. The yacht club has a crane for raising and lowering masts, for which a charge is made.

Shelter
The harbour enjoys good all round shelter.

Officials
Yacht club, Sport Nautique Valéricain, ☎ 22 26 91 64. The nearest customs office is in Abbeville. Police in the town.

Harbour dues
The harbour dues charged by the yacht club are reasonable.

Facilities
Water and electricity on the pontoons. The sailing club has excellent showers, toilets, a laundry room, bar and restaurant. Weather forecasts are posted up at the office. Fuel is available from filling stations, one on the Quai du Romerel, and the other on the

road to Abbeville. Both are at least half a mile away. Banks, post office and a reasonable selection of shops, including a couple of small supermarkets. Sunday market. Pharmacies, doctors, dentists, hospital. Two chandleries. Repair facilities for engines and hulls. There is a boatyard on the canal bank (just beyond the lock) which can lift boats from the water. Tourist information office. Restaurants.

Communications
Buses, taxis, car hire. Bicycles can be hired through the tourist information office. A narrow gauge steam railway links St-Valéry to Le Crotoy. It is now primarily intended for holidaymakers, and operates at weekends, on Wednesdays and on public holidays.

History
Perhaps the first episode in St-Valéry's history that the yachtsman will be aware of is William the Conqueror's departure from the port in 1066, en route for England. William's invasion fleet had originally gathered at Dives, and had set out for England from there. A fierce storm overtook the fleet, and those vessels which survived sought refuge at St-Valéry. A plaque on the wall of the salt warehouse on the quayside commemorates William's eventual departure for England.

St-Valéry (hence the town's name) founded an abbey here which flourished during the Middle Ages and was considered one of the finest Benedictine houses in northern France. Unfortunately, like many other monasteries and convents, it fell victim to the French Revolution. In 1791 the abbey lands were split into four lots and sold off. The abbey church was dismantled, but some of the abbey buildings, now privately owned, still exist.

Besides its abbey St-Valéry had a fortress, built originally in the ninth century and rebuilt in the thirteenth and fourteenth centuries. St-Valéry had been built on a rocky outcrop above the bay and was surrounded by a protective wall, with gateways and towers. Its commanding position on the Somme and its important port made St-Valéry a prime target for the various combatants in the Hundred Years War. In 1430 Joan of Arc passed through its gates as a prisoner of the English on her way to Rouen where she was burnt at the stake.

St-Valéry was an important port, with ships bringing goods from other French and European ports, and in later centuries from the Americas. Over the centuries it gained various privileges, for example becoming one of the main salt ports in the kingdom. The distribution and sale of salt were strictly controlled by the government, and it was heavily taxed. Salt had to be stored securely and a new warehouse for it was built at St-Valéry in 1736. This was the largest in France, being bigger than the warehouses in Caen, Le Havre, Honfleur and Nantes. It has been calculated that it could hold 19,500 tonnes of salt. This warehouse, now in a rather dilapidated state, stands on the quayside with the plaque commemorating William the Conqueror's departure for England.

The increase in the size of ships and the silting up of the port led to the decline of St-Valéry, which the construction of the canal did little to stop. Today it is a fishing and yachting centre.

To see

St-Valéry is an interesting town to wander around, but perhaps a little confusing. The tourist information office produces a helpful leaflet as well as a map to guide you round the main sights and walks.

The walled town with its towers, gates, and the church of St-Martin, lies beyond the street that the post office and shops are on. Amongst the main sights are the towers of William and Harold. The former has dungeons which, until the French Revolution, were the town's prison. The church of St-Martin perches on the town ramparts. It is an attractive and unpretentious church with flint and stone chequered walls. There is a model of a ship in one of the side chapels.

The remote chapel, seen up on the hillside as you approach St-Valéry was once the site of a hermitage. A simple chapel was built on the site and this was then replaced by the present flint and stone building.

Besides walking and sightseeing the town can offer the visitor golf, a casino, fishing, tennis, canoe hire, and trips on the steam railway or on the canal.

Etaples and Le Touquet

Position　Etaples 50°31′N 1°38′E
　　　　　Le Touquet 50°32′N 1°36′E

Charts Admiralty *2612, 2451*
　　　　Imray *C31*

General

The small havens of Etaples and Le Touquet lie in the shallow estuary of the River Canche. The estuary can only be approached in good weather and near high water. It is extremely dangerous to approach in strong winds.

Le Touquet is a fashionable resort complete with two casinos, racecourse, bistros and boutiques. It has a sailing club, but the club's moorings just inside the mouth of the estuary dry, and, as they are in an area of quicksand, are of limited use to the visiting yachtsman. Etaples on the other hand can offer a floating berth (1m at LWS) at a pontoon close to the centre of the town. The town is more down to earth, and life revolves around its fishing fleet, fish market and boat yards. If you yearn for the high life it is not all that far to the fleshpots of Le Touquet.

Tidal information

High water is approximately HW Dover −0010.

Tidal streams

To seaward of the entrance the N-going flood starts at HW Boulogne (or Dover) −0345, and reaches a maximum rate of 1¾ knots (springs). The south-going ebb starts at HW Boulogne +0230, and reaches a maximum of 1¾ knots (springs).

Minimum depths

Depths over the bar and in the channel are approximately 3m on springs and 1m on neaps at high water. The whole estuary dries completely, up to 2 miles offshore, at low water.

Approach

The Canche estuary should only be approached in good weather, and with good visibility. It is certainly hazardous even in moderate onshore winds.

A tall red lighthouse with a brown band, standing in the centre of Le Touquet, is conspicuous on an otherwise low, sandy and pine-clad coast. On the north shore of the estuary the white towers joined by a white wall of the British military cemetery show up well against the background of trees. The latticework light structure of Camiers, which has a sectored light, is difficult to see.

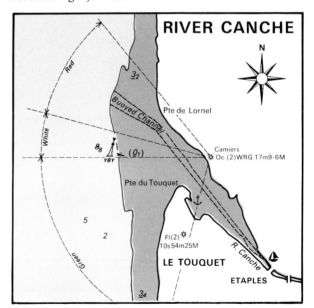

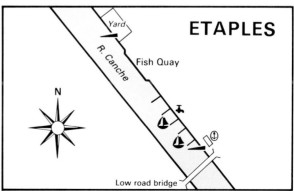

Looking downstream from Etaples marina towards the sea.

An unlit west cardinal buoy 2 miles northwest of Le Touquet lighthouse marks a wreck on the edge of the sands. The approach channel lies approximately 1 mile north of this buoy, but proceed with caution since the channel is constantly shifting. Unlit buoys mark both port and starboard sides of the channel. The buoys are moved as the channel changes. Within the estuary (above Le Touquet) the channel is constrained by training walls, marked by perches, instead of buoys.

It is important to keep within the channel, and wise to keep a beady eye on your echo sounder.

Timing

Entry is best attempted 1 hour before HW, and in daylight. To avoid the danger of being neaped, time your visit to coincide with rising tides.

Lights

Le Touquet Fl(2)10s54m25M
Camiers Oc(2)WRG.6s17m9-6M

Air radiobeacon

Le Touquet Aero RC *LT* 358 kHz 20M Cont
    50°32'·1N 1°35'·4E

Berth

Just inside the entrance lies Le Touquet sailing club, situated among sand dunes on the south shore. Their drying moorings for small yachts are easily seen. If you can dry out safely, it is possible to anchor near the moorings, out of the channel. The bottom consists of sand, with patches of stones. It may be dangerous to walk ashore at low tide, because of quicksand. Facilities in the vicinity of the yacht club are limited, but there is a good range of shops in Le Touquet.

Two miles upstream of Le Touquet, at the limit of navigation (a low road bridge prevents yachts with masts proceeding any further), lies the town of Etaples. Fishing boats lie alongside the quay. Visiting yachts should tie up at the pontoon berths further upstream. There is usually room for a visiting yacht here. Take care when approaching the pontoons; the current runs strongly (up to 5 knots) and the low bridge is uncomfortably close.

Harbour dues are collected by the tourist information office on the quayside at Etaples.

Shelter

Etaples offers excellent all round shelter.

Officials

Police in the towns. There is a customs post at Le Touquet airport. Yacht clubs at both Le Touquet and Etaples; Centre Nautique de la Canche Etaples-sur-Mer ☎ 21 94 74 26, Cercle Nautique du Touquet ☎ 21 05 12 77.

Facilities

At Etaples water and electricity are laid onto the pontoons. Toilets at the tourist information office. Petrol is available from the garage on the other side of the road, but the nearest garage selling diesel is some 10 minutes walk away on the road leading to Le Touquet. There is a good range of shops and restaurants close at hand, as well as a fish and vegetable market. On Sundays an interesting and lively flea market fills the nearby streets. Doctors and dentist. The fishing-boat yards can undertake repairs to hull and engine. Mobile cranes and travel-hoist.

Communications

Railway station, bus service, car hire and taxis. Flights to Paris and England from Le Touquet airport.

History

During the First World War Etaples was an important base for the British army with several military hospitals. Not surprisingly British troops referred to Etaples as 'Eat Apples'. On the outskirts of Etaples, on the road to Boulogne, there is the largest British military cemetery in northern France, with 11,300 British and Commonweaith graves. The cemetery is beautifully kept, and a visit here is a moving experience.

Le Touquet became a fashionable resort frequented by wealthy British visitors over a hundred years ago. It is still a fashionable resort, but the majority of holidaymakers are said to be Parisians. The resort's full name is Le Touquet-Paris-Plage.

To see

If you have the opportunity it is worth travelling inland to see the small walled town of Montreuil-sur-Mer. During the Middle Ages the Canche was considerably deeper and Montreuil had a flourishing port until the sixteenth century. Montreuil is now a sleepy town, perched on a hill with superb views over the valley. There are interesting old alleyways and streets. In the citadel is a list of men who died at the Battle of Agincourt in the fifteenth century. The local tourist information office has prepared some informative leaflets describing the town.

Boulogne

Position 50°45′N 1°34′E
Charts Admiralty *2451, 1892, 438* (plan)
          Imray *C31, C8*

General

Boulogne is France's most important fishing port. It is also busy with ferry and commercial shipping. For the British it is the most popular destination for a cross-Channel day trip. As you might guess, British visitors are well catered for. There is even an English pub!

The area around the harbour is a hubbub of traffic, with people hurrying, and tourist orientated bars and shops nearby. The old city perched up on the hillside and surrounded by thick medieval walls is in comparison a quiet refuge.

From the yachtsman's point of view the harbour can be entered whatever the weather or tide, and most facilities are available. Note, however, that strong winds from west to northwest can make entry difficult. The marina is on the basic side, and rather sordid, yet we found it the most expensive marina along this coast. There are only eight visitors' berths, so visiting yachts raft up, and drift back and forth in the wake of passing fishing craft. At a push, in bad weather and with work beckoning on Monday morning, it would be possible to leave a yacht here whilst the crew catch a ferry back home!

The pleasures ashore however more than make up for the inadequacies of the marina.

Tidal information

Standard port. HW approximately −0007 Dover.

Height of tide above chart datum
MHWS 9m, MHWN 7·2m, MLWN 2·8m, MLWS 1m

Tidal streams
At the entrance to the outer harbour, the tide flows as follows:
HW −0100 flood reaches 2·5 knots (springs) 030°
HW +0300 slack
HW +0500 ebb reaches 1·7 knots (springs) 200°

Minimum depths
Dredged to 4m below chart datum. There is a minimum depth of 2·9m at the visitors' berths. Note that parts of the harbour dry.

Approach

The approach to Boulogne outer harbour holds few dangers for yachts, apart from the constant ferry and hovercraft traffic. The breakwater of the large outer harbour can be seen from some distance, and the flow of ferry traffic will help you locate the entrance. The hovercraft port is outside to the south of the harbour.

Conspicuous features which help identify Boulogne are the cathedral cupola, the harbour breakwaters, and a tall commemorative pillar (the Colonne de la Grande Armée, the top of which is 140m above sea level) to the north of the town, east of the harbour entrance.

Note that the outer half of the north breakwater is permanently submerged. Only the platform marking its extremity is above water. Do not attempt to cross the submerged section of the breakwater.

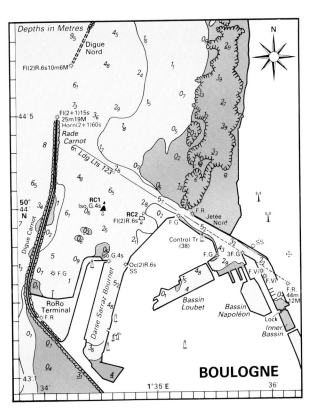

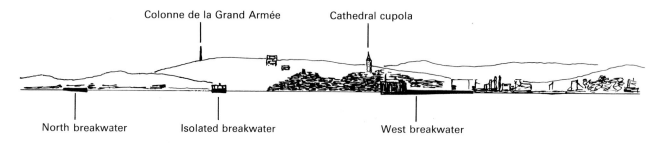

Colonne de la Grand Armée   Cathedral cupola

North breakwater   Isolated breakwater   West breakwater

Boulogne, 2M off, from cardinal buoy due west of entrance.

Beware of the tide running across the entrance. Once through the entrance do not steer directly for the inner harbour because of an extensive area which dries. Steer south until on the leading line, 123°. When on the leading line you can see directly through the inner breakwaters. Note that there is shallow water close north of the leading line. At night leading lights mark this approach. Within the inner harbour two wet docks lead off to starboard, but continue straight on, past the ferry berths, towards the pontoon berths on the west side of the inner basin.

Lights

The standard port traffic signals are exhibited from various places. These traffic signals are mainly intended for commercial vessels including ferries. Yachts may follow a ferry in or out of the harbour, but must keep out of its way.

Outer harbour
N breakwater Fl(2)R.6s10m6M
S breakwater Fl(2+1)15s25m19M Horn(2+1)60s
Inner harbour
N Jetty F.R.11m9M
S jetty F.G.17m5M Horn 30s
Leading lights in line 123°
Front 3F.G.4m5M
Rear DirF.R.44m12M

Radiobeacon

Directional 101° 289·6 kHz 5M 50°44′·4N 1°35′·8E:
   North = Morse A
   101° = steady note
   South = Morse N

Port radio

Port control uses VHF Ch 12.

Berth

The usual berth for a visiting yacht is at the marina, where the visitors' berths alongside the more northerly pontoon are marked. In the height of the season it is so crowded that visitors are rafted up outside the pontoons, perhaps 6 or more deep.

Large yachts (over 10m) will have to find space alongside the Quai Gambetta, amongst the fishing boats, after obtaining permission from the harbour-master.

Shelter

The yacht berths enjoy good all round shelter, although they are affected by surge from harbour traffic.

Officials

The marina office, situated on the quayside above the marina berths, carries out all procedures, and will give advice, ☎ 21 31 70 01. An up-to-date weather forecast is posted up at the office. Customs at 3, bd. Daunon, and police in the town. Boulogne has a British Consulate, Mr G.P.L. Stevens, who can be contacted at the Ferry Terminal, Boite Postale 27, Boulevard Chanzy, 62201 Boulogne-sur-Mer. ☎ 21 30 25 11.

Harbour dues

Marina fees are charged. We found this to be the most expensive port visited.

Facilities

Water on the pontoons. Fuel from a filling station on the Boulevard Gambetta, on the opposite side of the inner basin from the ferry berths and the marina. Large quantities of fuel can be delivered by tanker. Showers in the building which serves as the hovercraft waiting room, located on the west side of the Bassin Frédéric Sauvage. The key can be obtained, on payment of a deposit, from the marina office.

Banks, post office, an excellent selection of shops plus all the facilities of a city and a major ferry port are close to hand. There is a large Champion supermarket just southeast of the Bassin Frédéric Sauvage. Market on Wednesday and Saturday mornings at the Place Dalton. Fresh fish is sold every day on the Quai Gambetta. Laundrette at the eastern end of Rue Nationale, just beyond the railway bridge. Tourist information office. Hospital, doctors and dentists. Arrangements can be made to obtain duty-free goods. Chandleries. Repair facilities for hull, engine and sails. Mobile cranes. The grid near the yacht pontoons is not suitable for yachts. There is an excellent selection of restaurants to suit all pockets and tastes.

Communications

Ferries and hovercraft to Dover. Railway station and bus service. Car hire and taxis. Bicycles can be hired at the youth hostel at 36 Rue Porte Gayole.

The old town of Boulogne, up on the hill, overlooks the harbour.

History

In Roman times Boulogne was an important fortified settlement, and it was here that Julius Caesar assembled an army for his invasion of England in 55 BC. His army was transported in 800 vessels.

The strategic position of the Roman town was recognised by subsequent generations who continued to inhabit and fortify the site. The old town, perched up on a hillside overlooking the harbour, is still surrounded by medieval walls and towers, built in the thirteenth century. In places the ramparts are over 10 metres wide. Despite Boulogne's strong defences and being under the protection of the Virgin it was captured in 1544 by Henry VIII of England. Henry sold it back to the French Crown in 1550 for a mere 400,000 crowns.

In 1803 Napoléon Bonaparte used Boulogne as his base for the planned invasion of the British Isles, collecting together 2000 vessels, many of them flat bottomed barges. The Bassin Napoléon, to the west of the marina, was built to accommodate his invasion fleet. The invasion never took place, because the British navy under Nelson defeated the French fleet at Trafalgar. Despite Napoléon's fall from grace he is commemorated by a statue standing on top of a prominent column, the Colonne de la Grande Armée, which is situated northeast of the town. This column, perhaps France's answer to Nelson's Column, was erected in 1841.

During the eighteenth and nineteenth centuries Boulogne had a large English community, some living here because of their business, others to escape their debtors in England. In 1843 there were 5,000 British residents, out of a total population of 30,000.

During the Second World War Boulogne was occupied by the Nazis. The port area was heavily bombed by the Allies and approximately 5000 buildings were destroyed. The old town did not suffer so much damage, and fortunately there is still a lot to see within the walls.

To see

It is possible to walk right round the old town along the top of the city walls. There are superb views over the town and harbour from these ramparts. The walls and the castle were built in 1231 by Philippe Hurepel, Count of Boulogne. The castle has served as barracks for troops, a prison, and is due to be opened as a museum. One of its most famous prisoners was Louis Napoléon Bonaparte who was imprisoned here in 1840 after his attempted coup d'état failed.

Within the city walls there are a number of interesting buildings. Prominent among these are the cathedral, the town hall with its belfry, the library, the castle, and the so-called Palais Impérial.

The cathedral of Notre Dame was built in the nineteenth century on the site of an earlier church which had been destroyed by French revolutionaries. The generally Italian appearance of the exterior of the cathedral is reflected in the interior. The marble and mosaic altar was created in the workshops of the Vatican and erected in the cathedral in 1866. The cathedral has an eleventh-century crypt, where Edward II of England married Isabelle of France, which can be visited. A church was originally built on this site after a miracle occurred during the seventh century. A ship, bearing a statue of the Virgin, was mysteriously found on the top of the hill. It had no sails, and no sign of any crew. The site became a place of pilgrimage, even attracting royalty. A procession dedicated to the Vièrge Noire takes place every year on the second Sunday after 15th August.

The number of pilgrims coming to Boulogne was such that there was need of special accommodation. The Couvent des Annonciades, with its fine cloister, was built in the thirteenth century as a hostel for the pilgrims. Today it houses the municipal library.

The attractive town hall, built of red brick in the eighteenth century, contrasts with the solid grey stone thirteenth-century belfry. The belfry has a dungeon where prisoners were kept. It is possible to visit the belfry.

The eighteenth-century Hôtel Desandrouins, also known as the Palais Impérial, because Napoléon stayed here, is not open to the public.

There are fine panoramic views over the port from the sailors' chapel, the Calvaire des Marins. In the chapel are relics from shipwrecked vessels.

The Casa San Martine at 113 Grande Rue is where General San Martin, the liberator of Argentina, spent his last years. The house is open to the public on weekdays.

At the south end of the Boulevard Gambetta is a statue depicting Frédéric Sauvage with a propeller. Sauvage (1786–1857) was the first Frenchman to make use of the invention of the screw in steam ships.

Ambleteuse

Position 50°48′N 1°36′E
Chart Admiralty *1892*
 Imray *C8, C31*

The small town and former fishing port of Ambleteuse lies on the estuary of the river Slack, 5 miles north of Boulogne. It is easily identified by a small seventeenth-century castle (with a chimney) built on a rock just off the beach. In the town other prominent features are a belfry and a church.

Ambleteuse must once have been quite an important little port, and worth fortifying. James II landed at Ambleteuse when he fled from England in January 1698, and some of Napoléon's invasion fleet gathered here.

Today there is no port as such. The tubby fishing boats of the region are launched by tractor over the beach, and a sailing club races dinghies. The estuary is very shallow, and rock strewn. Rocky ledges fringe the beach and a number of dangerous wrecks lie within 1 mile.

Unfortunately it is no longer possible to make use of this ancient port since it is totally silted up.

Calais

Position 50°58′N 1°50′E
Charts Admiralty *1352* (plan), *1892, 2451*
 Imray *C8, C30*

General
Calais is the nearest port to England, and is extremely busy with cross-Channel ferry and hovercraft traffic. Yachts are however made welcome and are provided with excellent facilities. The yacht club showers are some of the best we have ever come across! If forced to spend a few days here, the time need not be wasted since there is so much to see and do in Calais.

Calais is a convenient port at which to enter the French canals.

Tidal information
Standard port. HW approximately +0025 Dover.

Height of tide above chart datum
MHWS 7m, MHWN 6m, MLWN 2m, MLWS 1m

Tidal streams
The tide sets across the harbour entrance, and should be guarded against when entering or leaving. On spring tides the tidal set can attain nearly 3 knots.

The east-going tidal stream just off the harbour entrance commences at HW Dover −0305; and the west-going stream commences at HW Dover

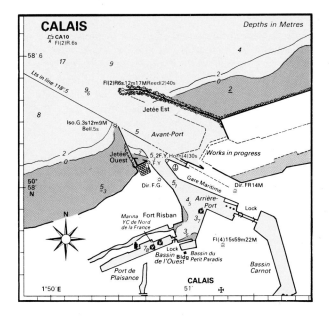

+0250. Further offshore the tidal streams change direction earlier.

On spring tides the rate is about 2¾ knots, whilst on neaps the rate is about 1½ knots. The east-going tidal direction is east-northeast, and the west-going stream west-southwest.

Beware of the possibility of the tide setting you off course and into danger when approaching the harbour.

Minimum depths
The outer part of the harbour is dredged to 8m, but certain parts of the harbour dry including the approaches to the yacht basin. A sea lock ensures that yachts in the Bassin de l'Ouest are afloat (in 7·8m) at all states of the tide.

Timing
Calais can be entered at any time, but entry into the floating yacht basin is only possible from 1½ hours before HW to ½ hour afterwards. At weekends and on public holidays the lock gate opens 2 hours before HW (morning and afternoon high tides only).

Approach
Calais can be identified by a tall white lighthouse in the town, and two distinctive belfries. Ferry traffic will help locate the entrance.

The main dangers in the approach to Calais are areas of shallows lying up to 2 miles offshore to the west, and the Ridens de la Rade, a sandbank lying approximately 1 mile north of Calais harbour entrance and parallel to the shore. The sandbank has depths of only 0·1m (LWS) in places. There is a dangerous wreck on the Ridens de la Rade.

In strong winds from northwest and northeast seas break on the sandbank. It is much safer to avoid entering Calais in these conditions.

The approach channel, entered from west, is well buoyed and lit. The best approach is made by steer-

ing initially for the west cardinal buoy *CA4*, leaving it to port, then following the edge of the buoyed channel to the harbour entrance. Note that there is an area of shallows off Bleriot-Plage, 1½ miles to the west of the harbour entrance. These shallows are marked by unlit buoys.

Beware of ferry traffic in the vicinity of Calais. Yachts are not allowed to enter or leave the harbour under sail.

Lights
Cap Gris Nez Fl.5s72m29M Siren 60s
Calais lighthouse Fl(4)15s59m23M RC
Calais W pierhead Iso.G.3s12m9M Bell 5s
Calais E pierhead Fl(2)R.6s12m17M Reed(2)40s

Radiobeacon
Calais lighthouse *CS* 305·7 kHz 20M Seq 5 Cont 50°57'·7N 1°51'·3E

Traffic signals
The standard port traffic signals are exhibited from the port office (a pyramid-shaped building near the east pier). The traffic signals are intended for all vessels, and a yacht should not enter against the lights. Yachts may, however, follow a ferry in or out of the harbour, but must keep out of its way. If dredging is in progress in the harbour this is indicated by a R light, below the normal traffic signals.

Port radio
Port control uses VHF Ch 12.

Berth
The best berth for a yacht, especially if staying for more than one tide, is in the Bassin de l'Ouest. Entry is controlled by a sea lock, which has a road bridge passing over it. The lock is open from HW −1½ hours until HW +½ hour. The bridge however only opens at specific times to allow the passage of vessels. 10 minutes before the bridge is due to open an orange light is exhibited on the lock. A green light is the go-ahead to enter the basin, whilst a red light allows departure.

Berth at the yacht club as directed by the club officials. You will most likely be expected to tie up at the visitors' pontoon to starboard. Larger yachts may be directed to a berth on the opposite side of the basin. The yacht club is busy and visiting boats can be three or more deep alongside the pontoon.

The berth on the opposite side of the basin is cheaper than at the yacht club itself (where all dues are payable), is closer to the town, and hence further from the yacht club facilities. It also lacks any security. This quayside is used by commercial traffic and you may be asked to move to allow the berthing of a freighter.

A number of mooring buoys are provided near the lock in the Arrière-Port for the use of vessels waiting to enter the Bassin de l'Ouest. Vessels may moor at one of these buoys for a maximum of 24 hours. Beware of buoys just below the surface; it is

The visitors' berth at Calais yacht club, with the nearby club-house.

some time since these buoys were serviced, some have sunk and some may lurk just below the surface to trap the unwary. If you do not wish to pass through the sea lock, anchor in the vicinity of the buoys, rigging a tripping line.

Yachts can also berth alongside the quay northeast of the Bassin du Petit Paradis, but the yacht should not be left unattended here. This quay is used by fishing boats. Note that the more southerly part of this quay dries, and that the bottom is foul.

To enter the French canals

If you are able to lower your own mast (or don't have one) go straight to the Bassin Carnot, the commercial dock. Otherwise enter the Bassin de l'Ouest and have the yacht club crane lower your mast. Charges for this are reasonable.

To enter the Carnot lock it is simplest to walk along to the lock-keeper's office at the Bassin Carnot to ask when they will lock you into the docks. This lock operates between HW −1½hrs and HW +¾hr. Lock in and follow your nose through the string of interconnecting docks. At the far end you will arrive at the double lock leading to the Canal de St-Omer. You may have difficulty finding the lock-keeper here – we did! He was having a long lunch break.

Shelter

The Bassin de l'Ouest enjoys good all round shelter. However in strong northwest and northeast winds a considerable surge affects the visitors' berths whenever the lock gates are open (up to 2½ hours per tide). We suffered a broken cleat and chafed ropes when lying here during a northwesterly gale. Take particular care to secure strongly and guard against chafe if leaving a yacht and catching a ferry home.

Officials

The officials at the yacht club are a good source of information, as are those at the harbourmaster's office. The customs office is now at Rue Lamy. Police in the town. Port de Plaisance (Bassin Ouest) ☎ 21 34 55 23. The British Consul in Calais is based at Readicut (France) SA, Route de Dunkerque, ☎ 21 96 46 94 and 21 96 33 76.

Harbour dues

The yacht club administers all the berths in the yacht basin, and charges moderate fees. It also displays a list of those who left without paying!

Facilities

Water and fuel from the yacht club in the Bassin de l'Ouest. The yacht club also has excellent showers and a bar, and will take orders for duty-free goods. There is a small crane at the yacht club for lowering and raising masts, and a mobile crane for lifting boats in and out of the water. Repairs to engine, hull and sails are possible.

Banks, post office (note that Poste Restante mail is held at the main post office, not the one nearest the harbour). Open-air market at Place Crèvecoeur on Thursdays and Saturdays. There is also a covered market on Wednesdays and Saturdays. Fresh fish is sold on the quayside on the south side of the harbour. Calais has an excellent selection of shops including a hypermarket on the eastern outskirts. Laundrette in Rue des Thermes. Hospital, doctors and dentists. Tourist information office. Good selection of restaurants. All the facilities of a major ferry port.

Communications

Ferries and hovercraft to Dover. Railway station and bus service. Airport. Car hire and taxis.

History

Most of us remember being told as school children that Calais once belonged to England, but we don't always recall the details!

The English conquest of Calais occurred during the Hundred Years War, a bitter struggle waged in the fourteenth century between the English and the French. After the English victory at the battle of Crécy in September 1346 Edward III laid siege to Calais. He referred to Calais as that 'nest of pirates'; the attacks on English trading vessels carried out by Calais sailors had infuriated him. Calais resisted the siege for nearly a year, but in August 1347 conditions were so bad that the town surrendered to Edward.

To save Calais and its inhabitants from Edward's wrath six prominent citizens offered themselves to the English king as a ransom. They came out to the English barefoot, nooses already around their necks, and carrying the town keys. Their lives and the town were only spared after Edward's pregnant queen, Philippa, went down on her knees and begged the king to be merciful. The heroism of these six men is depicted in Rodin's famous statue which stands outside the town hall.

Calais continued to be an important English possession for just over 200 years. It was from Calais that Henry VIII set out to meet the French monarch, François I, at the legendary Field of the Cloth of Gold. At this meeting both kings tried to outdo the other in displays of wealth and chivalry.

In 1558 30,000 French troops under the leadership of the Duc de Guise finally recaptured Calais. The loss of Calais was such a blow to the English that Queen Mary Tudor said that the name 'Calais' would be found graven on her heart when she died. French control of Calais was lost again for a brief period between 1596 and 1598 when Spanish troops captured and occupied the town.

From the earliest times Calais has been an important ferry port, and it has seen many famous passengers. Richard the Lionheart landed at Calais in 1189 when he was on his way to the Crusades. The young widow of François II, Mary Queen of Scots, sailed from Calais in 1561 to take up her throne in Scotland. A few centuries later in 1814 the people of Calais gave an enthusiastic welcome to Louis XVIII when he landed at the port on his way to Paris to assume the French crown. In the same year Lord Nelson's mistress, Emma Lyons (Lady Hamilton) died in poverty in Calais. Another famous English exile who lived for a while in Calais was Beau Brummell, the so-called 'King of Fashion'. He spent the years 1817 to 1830 here.

In the eighteenth century the Dover to Calais packet was the only regular passenger service from England to France and Europe. This route was the first in the world to use a steam ship. The first steam ferry, the *Rob-Roy*, entered service in 1821.

In 1816 three Nottingham men smuggled machinery for making lace out of Britain, and established a lace industry in Calais. Local lace can be bought in the town, and there is a permanent exhibition in the town museum.

Calais played an important role during the First World War when English troops and arms were landed at the port. It suffered heavy bombing as a result, but was not occupied by German troops. In the Second World War Calais was captured by the Germans, who based their North Sea naval headquarters here.

To see

Despite severe damage during the last two wars Calais is not a city of concrete and glass. Many of the historic buildings have been restored. The main places of interest are as follows:

The town hall (the Hôtel de Ville) is one of those buildings you either love or hate. It was built in 1927 in a colourful neo-Flemish Renaissance style, with a most distinctive belfry which is 75m high. The Hôtel de Ville has stained glass windows and paintings depicting scenes from Calais' past, including Edward III's capture of the town and the Duc de Guise's victory in 1558. In front of the Hôtel de Ville is Rodin's famous sculpture showing the six

Rodin's famous statue depicting the Burghers of Calais.

burghers of Calais, complete with nooses around their necks.

Calais has two museums. The war museum is housed in the Nazi *blockhaus* which used to be the German navy's telephone exchange. The town museum has exhibits from the two hundred years of English rule, a display of Calais lace, as well as paintings.

The oldest parts of the church of Notre Dame date from the thirteenth century. The church is unique in that it is believed to be the only example of the English perpendicular style of architecture on the continent. In 1921 Charles de Gaulle married Yvonne Vendroux in this church.

The watchtower in the Place d'Armes was built in approximately 1224 on the orders of Philippe, earl of Boulogne. The tower was restored in 1806 and used as a lighthouse until 1848.

The citadel was built between 1560 and 1571 on the foundations of an earlier medieval castle. It was further improved in the seventeenth century by the famous army architect, Vauban. The citadel now houses a sports stadium and gardens.

The ruined Fort Risban overlooking the harbour was built on the remains of the English 'Lancaster Tower' in the sixteenth century.

Besides sightseeing in and around Calais the nearby beaches will have their attractions, especially for those with children. In addition day trips to Dover are very popular.

Appendix

I. TIDAL STREAM DIAGRAMS

The figures shown against the arrows are the mean spring and neap rates in tenths of a knot. Thus 07,15 -mean spring rate 0:7 knots, mean neap rate 1:5 knots.

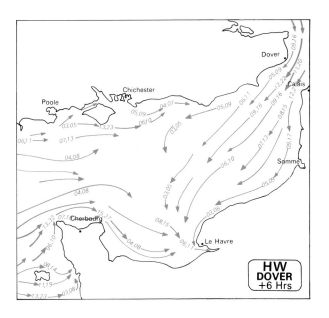

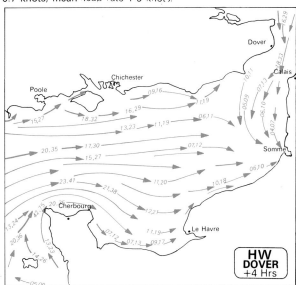

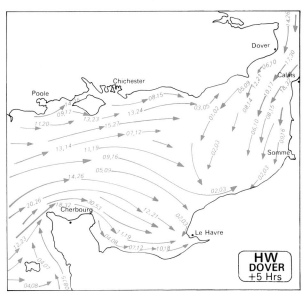

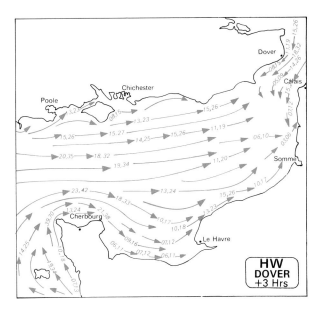

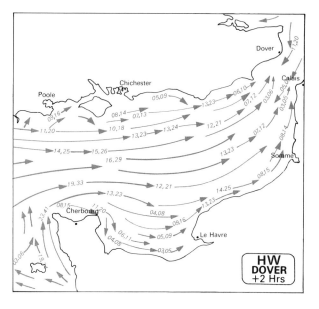

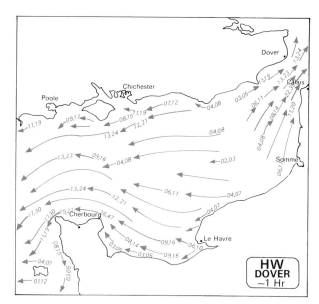

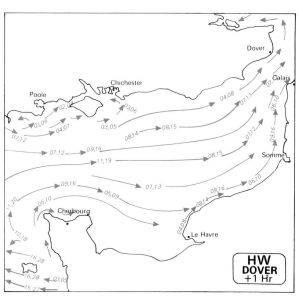

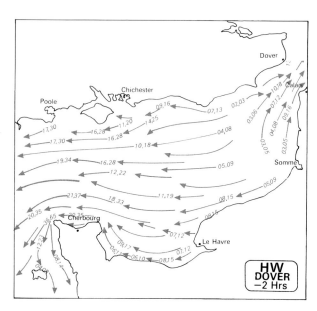

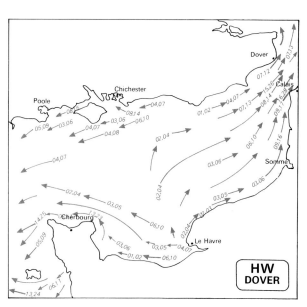

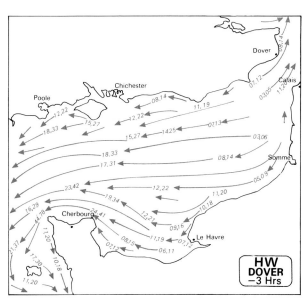

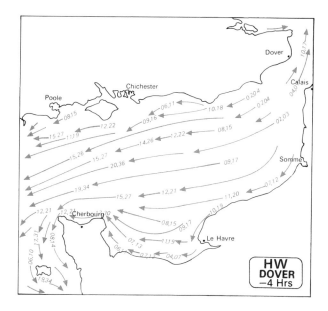

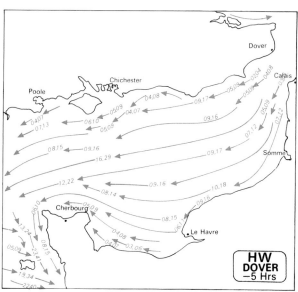

II. CHARTS

Admiralty

323	Dover strait – eastern part	75,000
438	Boulogne	10,000
1106	Approaches to Cherbourg	50,000
1349	Ports in Normandy:	
	Ouistreham: Port de Caen: Barfleur:	
	Deauville-Trouville	15,000
	Saint Vaast La Hougue: Courseulles	20,000
	Canal de Caen	50,000
1352	Ports on the north coast of France:	
	Le Tréport: Fécamp: Calais	250,000
1821	Asnelles to Villers, including	
	Rade de Caen	45,400
1892	Dover Strait – western part	75,000
2073	Pte de Barfleur to Courseulles	73,200
2146	Approaches to Le Havre	60,000
2147	Approaches to Dieppe	50,000
2450	Anvil point to Beachy head	150,000
2451	Newhaven to Calais	150,000
2602	Cherbourg	10,000
2612	Cap d'Antifer to Pte du Haut Blanc	150,000
2613	Cherbourg to Cap d'Antifer	150,000
2656	English channel – central part	325,000
2669	The Channel islands and adjacent	
	coast of France	150,000
2990	Le Havre and approaches to la Seine	15,000
2994	La Seine – Honfleur to Rouen	44,600

Imray

C8	North Foreland to Beachy Head and Boulogne (Pegwell Bay. Ramsgate. Dover. Folkestone. Rye. Calais. Boulogne)	115,000
C12	Eastern English Channel Passage Chart (Radiobeacons. Lights. Tides)	400,000
C30	Thames to Holland and Belgium Harwich and North Foreland to Hoek van Holland and Calais. (Dunkerque. Oostende. Zeebrugge. Flushing. Nieuwpoort. Breskens Blankenberge)	182,000
C31	Beachy Head to Boulogne and Le Havre (Dieppe. Fécamp. St-Valéry-en-Caux. Le Havre. Boulogne. Le Tréport)	187,000
C32	Baie de Seine. Le Havre to Cherbourg (Ouistreham. Cherbourg. St-Vaast-la-Hougue. Courseulles-sur-Mer. Port-en-Bessin. Trouville. Barfleur. Baie du Grand Vey. Arromanches. Dives. Le Havre Yacht Harbour. Grandcamp-Maisy)	155,000
C33A	Channel Islands (North) (St Peter Port. Omonville. Goury. Portbail. Dielette. Carteret. Gorey. Alderney. Beaucette Marina. Creux Harbour. St Sampson)	120,000

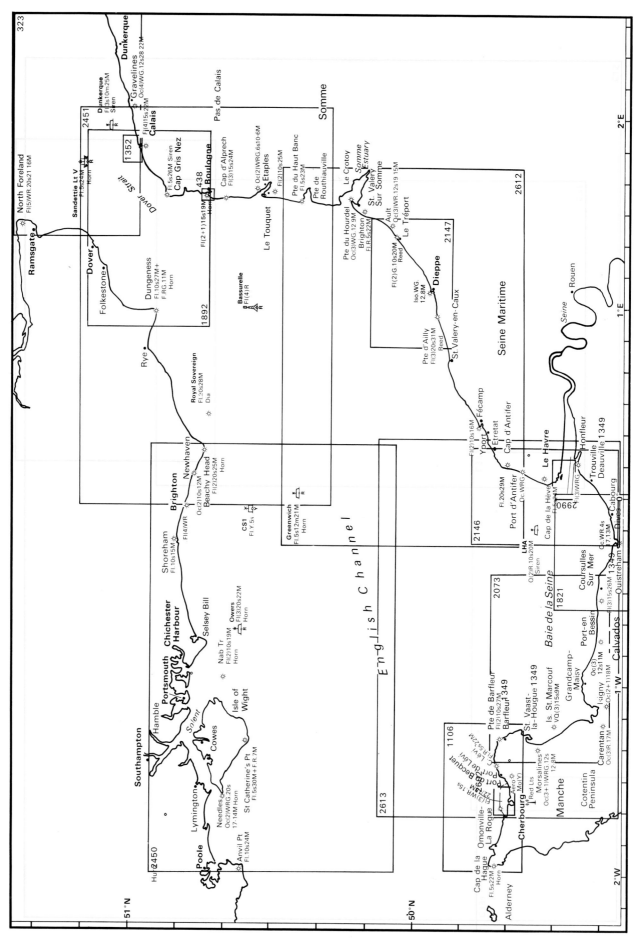

III. GLOSSARY

For French terms used in weather forecasts and for numerals see page 7.

French	English
abri, abrité	shelter, sheltered
abricot	apricots
accastillage	ship chandlery
agneau	lamb
aigu(e)	pointed, sharp
aiguille	needle
algue	seaweed
alimentation	grocer
amer	landmark, beacon
amont	upstream, landward
anse	bay, cove, creek
appontement	landing stage
argile	clay
arrière-port	inner port
asséchant	drying
au revoir	goodbye
aubergine	aubergine
aujourd'hui	today
aval	downstream, seaward
avant-port	outer harbour
azur	blue
baie	bay
balise	beacon
banc	bank
banque	bank
barre	bar
bas(e)	low
basse	shoal
bassin	basin, dock
batterie	battery
beurre	butter
bibliothèque	library
bijouterie	jeweller
biscuits	biscuits
blanc(he)	white
blanchisserie	laundry
bleu(e)	blue
boeuf	beef
bois	woods
bonjour	good afternoon
bonjour	good morning
bonne nuit	good night
bonsoir	good evening
bouche	mouth of river or channel
boucherie	butcher
boue	mud
bouée	buoy
boulangerie	bakery
brisant, brisants	shoal, breakers
brise-lames	breakwater
bureau de port	harbour office
bureau de port, capitainerie	port office
bureau de poste, la poste, PTT	post office
butte	knoll, mound
câble aérien	overhead cable
café	coffee
calanque	cove, inlet
cale	ramp, slip, hard
canal	canal, channel
canot de sauvetage	lifeboat
cap	cape, headland
capitaine de port	harbourmaster
capitainerie	port/harbour office
carburant	fuel, petrol
carénage	scrubbing berth
carottes	carrots
carré(e)	square
carrière	quarry
champ-de-tir	firing range
chantier	dockyard
chantier navale	ship/yacht yard
charcuterie	butcher (cooked meats)
château	castle, mansion
chaussée	bank, causeway
chemin de fer (SNCF, SNRP)	railway
chenal	channel
chocolat	chocolate
citron	lemon
clocher	steeple, belfry
coiffeur	hairdresser
col	mountain pass, neck
colline	hill
comment?	how?
concombre	cucumber
conduite	pipeline
confiture	jam
cordonnier	shoemaker, cobbler
corps mort	mooring
côte	coast
courant	current, stream
couvent	convent
crête	ridge, crest
crique	creek
crochet scellé	ringbolt
croix	cross
d'accord	OK
darse	basin
de rien	it's nothing
débarcadère	wharf, landing place
demain	tomorrow
détroit	strait, narrow
déversoir	weir
digue	mole, breakwater
dimanche	Sunday
douane	customs
douches	showers
draguer	to dredge
drapier	draper
droguerie	chemist
droit	right
dur(e)	hard
eau	water
écluse	lock (of a canal basin)
écuiel	shoal, reef
église	church
enceinte militaire	military area
épave	wreck
épi	short mole, spur
épicerie	grocer
est	east
estuaire	estuary
étang	lake, lagoon
étier	navigable creek
falaise	cliff
farine	flour
fermé	closed

feu	light	*méridional(e)*	southern
fleuve	river, stream	*meubles*	furniture
forêt	forest	*miel*	honey
fosse	ditch, a deep	*milieu*	middle
fromage	cheese	*môle*	mole, pier
fruits et légumes	greengrocer	*mont, montagne*	mount, mountain
		mort eau	neap tide
galets	shingle	*mouillage*	anchorage
gare	station	*mouillage interdit*	anchoring prohibited
gasoil	fuel	*moulin*	mill
gauche	left	*mur*	wall
gendarmerie	police station	*musoir*	mole or pierhead
glace	ice		
golfe	gulf	*neuf(ve)*	new
goulet	inlet	*nez*	nose, promontory
grand(e)	big, great	*noir(e)*	black
grau	channel	*non*	no
gravier	gravel	*nord*	north
grèv	sandy beach	*nouveau(el) (elle)*	new
gris(e)	grey		
gros(se)	large, coarse	*occidental(e)*	western
grue	crane	*oeufs*	eggs
guérite	watchtower, turret	*oignons*	onions
guet	watch-house	*oranges*	oranges
		oriental(e)	eastern
halage	towing	*où?*	where?
hampe	pole beacon	*ouest*	west
haricots	beans	*oui*	yes
haut(e)	high, tall	*ouvert*	open
haut-fond	shoal		
havre	harbour	*pain*	bread
Hôtel de Ville	town hall	*papetier*	stationer
huile	oil	*parcage, parking*	car park
huître	oyster	*pardon*	excuse me
hutte	hut, cottage	*passagères*	visitors' berths
		passe	passage, pass
île	island, isle	*pâtisserie*	cake shop
îlot	islet	*pêches*	peaches
immobilière	estate agent	*pertuis*	opening or strait
interdire	to forbid	*petit(e)*	small
interdit	forbidden	*phare*	lighthouse
isthmi	isthmus	*pic*	peak
		pierre	stone
jaune	yellow	*pieux*	stakes, piles
jetée	jetty	*pignon*	gable
jeudi	Thursday	*pin*	pine or fir tree
journaux	newsagent	*piscine*	swimming pool
		plage	beach, shore
lac	lake	*plaine*	plain
lait	milk	*plat(e)*	flat, level
laiterie	dairy	*plateau*	shoal
large	broad, wide	*plongeoir*	diving stage
laverie	laundrette	*pointe*	point
librairie	book shop	*poisson*	fish
lundi	Monday	*pommes*	apples
		pommes de terre	potatoes
magasin	shop	*pompage*	pumping station
mairie	town hall	*pont*	bridge, deck
maison	house	*pont dormant*	fixed bridge
marais	swamp, marsh	*pont mobile*	moving bridge
marché	market	*pont tournant*	swing bridge
mardi	Tuesday	*port*	port, harbour
marée	tide	*poulet*	chicken
marine	marine	*presqu'île*	peninsula
mât	mast	*prise d'eau*	water point
mécanicien	mechanic	*projeté*	intended
melon	melon	*pylône*	pylon
mer	sea		
merci	thank you	*quai*	quay, wharf
mercredi	Wednesday	*quai d'accueil*	arrivals/reception quay
		quand?	when?

rade	road, roadstead	basin, dock	*bassin, darse*
récif	reef	battery	*batterie*
redoute	redoubt, fort	bay	*baie*
réservé	reserved	bay, cove, creek	*anse*
rivière	river	beach, shore	*plage*
riz	rice	beacon	*balise*
roche	rock	beans	*haricots*
rocher	rock, above water	beef	*boeuf*
rond(e)	round	big, great	*grand(e)*
rouge	red	biscuits	*biscuits*
roux, rousse	reddish	black	*noir(e)*
ruisseau	rivulet	blue	*azur, bleu(e)*
		book shop	*librairie*
s'il vous plait	please	bread	*pain*
sable	sand	breakwater	*brise-lames*
sablon	fine sand	bridge, deck	*pont*
saline	salt water lagoon, saltworks	broad, wide	*large*
samedi	Saturday	buoy	*bouée*
sel	salt	butcher	*boucherie*
septentrional(e)	northern	butcher (cooked meats)	*charcuterie*
ship chandler	yacht chandler	butter	*beurre*
sommet	summit		
sucre	sugar	cake shop	*pâtisserie*
sud	south	canal, channel	*canal*
Syndicat d'Initiative (SI)	information office	cape, headland	*cap*
		car park	*parcage, parking*
tabac	tobacconist	carrots	*carottes*
tailleur	tailor	castle, mansion	*château*
taxi	taxi	channel	*chenal, grau*
terre-plein	levelled ground, platform	cheese	*fromage*
tertre	hillock, knoll	chemist	*droguerie*
tête	head	chicken	*poulet*
thé	tea	chocolate	*chocolat*
tomates	tomatoes	church	*église*
torchère	flare	clay	*argile*
torrent	stream, torrent	cliff	*falaise*
tour	tower	closed	*fermé*
tourelle	small tower, turret	coast	*côte*
travaux projetés	works in progress	coffee	*café*
traverse	shallow ridge or bar	convent	*couvent*
		cove, inlet	*calanque*
vagues	waves	crane	*grue*
val	narrow valley	creek	*crique*
vallée	valley	cross	*croix*
vasière	mudbank, mudflat	cucumber	*concombre*
vedette	ferry	current, stream	*courant*
vendredi	Friday	customs	*douane*
vert(e)	green		
viande	meat	dairy	*laiterie*
vieil, vieille, vieux	old, ancient	ditch, a deep	*fosse*
village	village	diving stage	*plongeoir*
ville	town	dockyard	*chantier*
vin	wine	downstream, seaward	*aval*
vins	wine shop	draper	*drapier*
vive eau	spring tide	drying	*asséchant*
voilier	sailmaker		
		east	*est*
English	**French**	eastern	*oriental(e)*
anchorage	*mouillage*	eggs	*oeufs*
anchoring prohibited	*mouillage interdit*	estate agent	*immobilière*
apples	*pommes*	estuary	*estuaire*
apricots	*abricot*	excuse me	*pardon*
arrivals/reception quay	*quai d'accueil*		
aubergine	*aubergine*	ferry	*vedette*
		fine sand	*sablon*
bakery	*boulangerie*	firing range	*champ-de-tir*
bank	*banc*	fish	*poisson*
bank	*banque*	fixed bridge	*pont dormant*
bank, causeway	*chaussée*	flare	*torchère*
bar	*barre*	flat, level	*plat(e)*

flour	*farine*	marine	*marine*
forbidden	*interdit*	market	*marché*
forest	*forêt*	mast	*mât*
Friday	*vendredi*	meat	*viande*
fuel	*gasoil*	mechanic	*mécanicien*
fuel, petrol	*carburant*	melon	*melon*
furniture	*meubles*	middle	*milieu*
		military area	*enceinte militaire*
gable	*pignon*	milk	*lait*
good afternoon	*bonjour*	mill	*moulin*
good evening	*bonsoir*	mole or pierhead	*musoir*
good morning	*bonjour*	mole, breakwater	*digue*
good night	*bonne nuit*	mole, pier	*môle*
goodbye	*au revoir*	Monday	*lundi*
gravel	*gravier*	mooring	*corps mort*
green	*vert(e)*	mount, mountain	*mont, montagne*
greengrocer	*fruits et légumes*	mountain pass, neck	*col*
grey	*gris(e)*	mouth of river or channel	*bouche*
grocer	*alimentation*	moving bridge	*pont mobile*
grocer	*épicerie*	mud	*boue*
gulf	*golfe*	mudbank, mudflat	*vasière*
hairdresser	*coiffeur*	narrow valley	*val*
harbour	*havre*	navigable creek	*étier*
harbour office	*bureau de port*	neap tide	*mort eau*
harbourmaster	*capitaine de port*	needle	*aiguille*
hard	*dur(e)*	new	*neuf(ve)*
head	*tête*	new	*nouveau(el) (elle)*
high, tall	*haut(e)*	newsagent	*journaux*
hill	*colline*	no	*non*
hillock, knoll	*tertre*	north	*nord*
honey	*miel*	northern	*septentrional(e)*
house	*maison*	nose, promontory	*nez*
how?	*comment?*		
hut, cottage	*hutte*	oil	*huile*
		OK	*d'accord*
ice	*glace*	old, ancient	*vieil, vieille, vieux*
information office	*Syndicat d'Initiative (SI)*	onions	*oignons*
inlet	*goulet*	open	*ouvert*
inner port	*arrière-port*	opening or strait	*pertuis*
intended	*projeté*	oranges	*oranges*
island, isle	*île*	outer harbour	*avant-port*
islet	*îlot*	overhead cable	*câble aérien*
isthmus	*isthmi*	oyster	*huître*
it's nothing	*de rien*		
		passage, pass	*passe*
jam	*confiture*	peaches	*pêches*
jetty	*jetée*	peak	*pic*
jeweller	*bijouterie*	peninsula	*presqu'île*
		pine or fir tree	*pin*
knoll, mound	*butte*	pipeline	*conduite*
		plain	*plaine*
lake	*lac*	please	*s'il vous plait*
lake, lagoon	*étang*	point	*pointe*
lamb	*agneau*	pointed, sharp	*aigu(e)*
landing stage	*appontement*	pole beacon	*hampe*
landmark, beacon	*amer*	police station	*gendarmerie*
large, coarse	*gros(se)*	port office	*bureau de port, capitainerie*
laundrette	*laverie*	port, harbour	*port*
laundry	*blanchisserie*	port/harbour office	*capitainerie*
left	*gauche*	post office	*bureau de poste, la poste, PTT*
lemon	*citron*		
levelled ground, platform	*terre-plein*	potatoes	*pommes de terre*
library	*bibliothèque*	pumping station	*pompage*
lifeboat	*canot de sauvetage*	pylon	*pylône*
light	*feu*		
lighthouse	*phare*	quarry	*carrière*
lock (of a canal basin)	*écluse*	quay, wharf	*quai*
low	*bas(e)*		

railway	*chemin de fer (SNCF)*	to forbid	*interdire*
ramp, slip, hard	*cale*	tobacconist	*tabac*
red	*rouge*	today	*aujourd'hui*
reddish	*roux, rousse*	tomatoes	*tomates*
redoubt, fort	*redoute*	tomorrow	*demain*
reef	*récif*	tower	*tour*
reserved	*réservé*	towing	*halage*
rice	*riz*	town	*ville*
ridge, crest	*crête*	town hall	*Hôtel de Ville*
right	*droit*	town hall	*mairie*
ringbolt	*crochet scellé*	Tuesday	*mardi*
river	*rivière*		
river, stream	*fleuve*	upstream, landward	*amont*
rivulet	*ruisseau*		
road, roadstead	*rade*	valley	*vallée*
rock	*roche*	village	*village*
rock, above water	*rocher*	visitors' berths	*passagères*
round	*rond(e)*		
		wall	*mur*
sailmaker	*voilier*	watch-house	*guet*
salt	*sel*	watchtower, turret	*guérite*
salt water lagoon, saltworks	*saline*	water	*eau*
sand	*sable*	water point	*prise d'eau*
sandy beach	*grève*	waves	*vagues*
Saturday	*samedi*	Wednesday	*mercredi*
scrubbing berth	*carénage*	weir	*déversoir*
sea	*mer*	west	*ouest*
seaweed	*algue*	western	*occidental(e)*
shallow ridge or bar	*traverse*	wharf, landing place	*débarcadère*
shelter, sheltered	*abri, abrité*	when?	*quand?*
shingle	*galets*	where?	*où?*
ship chandlery	*accastillage*	white	*blanc(he)*
ship/yacht yard	*chantier navale*	wine	*vin*
shoal	*basse*	wine shop	*vins*
shoal	*haut-fond*	woods	*bois*
shoal	*plateau*	works in progress	*travaux projetés*
shoal, breakers	*brisant, brisants*	wreck	*épave*
shoal, reef	*écuiel*		
shoemaker, cobbler	*cordonnier*	yacht chandler	*ship chandler*
shop	*magasin*	yellow	*jaune*
short mole, spur	*épi*	yes	*oui*
showers	*douches*		
small	*petit(e)*		
small tower, turret	*tourelle*		
south	*sud*		
southern	*méridional(e)*		
spring tide	*vive eau*		
square	*carré(e)*		
stakes, piles	*pieux*		
station	*gare*		
stationer	*papetier*		
steeple, belfry	*clocher*		
stone	*pierre*		
strait, narrow	*détroit*		
stream, torrent	*torrent*		
sugar	*sucre*		
summit	*sommet*		
Sunday	*dimanche*		
swamp, marsh	*marais*		
swimming pool	*piscine*		
swing bridge	*pont tournant*		
tailor	*tailleur*		
taxi	*taxi*		
tea	*thé*		
thank you	*merci*		
Thursday	*jeudi*		
tide	*marée*		
to dredge	*draguer*		

IV. CONVERSION TABLES

metres–feet

m	ft/m	ft
0·3	1	3·3
0·6	2	6·6
0·9	3	9·8
1·2	4	13·1
1·5	5	16·4
1·8	6	19·7
2·1	7	23·0
2·4	8	26·2
2·7	9	29·5
3·0	10	32·8
6·1	20	65·6
9·1	30	98·4
12·2	40	131·2
15·2	50	164·0
30·5	100	328·1

centimetres–inches

cm	in/cm	in
2·5	1	0·4
5·1	2	0·8
7·6	3	1·2
10·2	4	1·6
12·7	5	2·0
15·2	6	2·4
17·8	7	2·8
20·3	8	3·1
22·9	9	3·5
25·4	10	3·9
50·8	20	7·9
76·2	30	11·8
101·6	40	15·7
127·0	50	19·7
254·0	100	39·4

metres–fathoms–feet

m	fathoms	ft
0·9	0·5	3
1·8	1	6
3·7	2	12
5·5	3	18
7·3	4	24
9·1	5	30
11·0	6	36
12·8	7	42
14·6	8	48
16·5	9	54
18·3	10	60
36·6	20	120
54·9	30	180
73·2	40	240
91·4	50	300

kilometres–statute miles

km	M/km	M
1·6	1	0·6
3·2	2	1·2
4·8	3	1·9
6·4	4	2·5
8·0	5	3·1
9·7	6	3·7
11·3	7	4·3
12·9	8	5·0
14·5	9	5·6
16·1	10	6·2
32·2	20	12·4
48·3	30	18·6
64·4	40	24·9
80·5	50	31·1
120·7	75	46·6
160·9	100	62·1
402·3	250	155·3
804·7	500	310·7
1609·3	1000	621·4

kilograms–pounds

kg	lb/kg	lb
0·5	1	2·2
0·9	2	4·4
1·4	3	6·6
1·8	4	8·8
2·3	5	11·0
2·7	6	13·2
3·2	7	15·4
3·6	8	17·6
4·1	9	19·8
4·5	10	22·0
9·1	20	44·1
13·6	30	66·1
18·1	40	88·2
22·7	50	110·2
34·0	75	165·3
45·4	100	220·5
113·4	250	551·2
226·8	500	1102·3
453·6	1000	2204·6

litres–gallons

l	gal/l	gal
4·5	1	0·2
9·1	2	0·4
13·6	3	0·7
18·2	4	0·9
22·7	5	1·1
27·3	6	1·3
31·8	7	1·5
36·4	8	1·8
40·9	9	2·0
45·5	10	2·2
90·9	20	4·4
136·4	30	6·6
181·8	40	8·8
227·3	50	11·0
341·0	75	16·5
454·6	100	22·0
1136·5	250	55·0
2273·0	500	110·0
4546·1	1000	220·0

Index